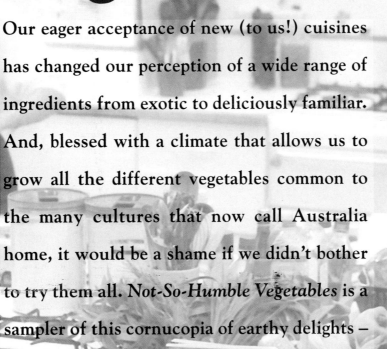

# Not-so-humble
# vegetables

Our eager acceptance of new (to us!) cuisines
has changed our perception of a wide range of
ingredients from exotic to deliciously familiar.
And, blessed with a climate that allows us to
grow all the different vegetables common to
the many cultures that now call Australia
home, it would be a shame if we didn't bother
to try them all. *Not-So-Humble Vegetables* is a
sampler of this cornucopia of earthy delights –
reach into our recipe garden and discover the
wonderful world of the tastes and textures of
fresh vegetables.

*Pamela Clark*

**FOOD EDITOR**

# Nutrition guide

*Vegetables are valued for more than just their taste and variety: their nutritional content plays an important part in your daily diet.*

**NOTES:**
- We have not included fat or protein amounts because they are negligible in vegetables (except for the avocado's high mono-unsaturated fat content).
- Measurements are for 100g of peeled and trimmed raw vegetable.
- Folate figures are unavailable in Australia at time of publication. However, folate is particularly important for women prior to and during pregnancy. Green vegetables, chickpeas and parsnips are excellent sources of folate.

| NUTRIENTS | Artichoke, globe | Artichoke, jerusalem | Asian vegetables (choy sum) | Asparagus | Avocado | Beans, broad | Beans, green | Beetroot | Broccoli | Brussels sprouts | Cabbage | Capsicum, green | Capsicum, red | Carrot | Cauliflower | Celeriac | Celery | Choko | Corn, sweet |
|---|---|---|---|---|---|---|---|---|---|---|---|---|---|---|---|---|---|---|---|
| **ENERGY (kj)** | 80 | 93 | 48 | 71 | 879 | 173 | 87 | 173 | 101 | 114 | 72 | 67 | 104 | 103 | 80 | 119 | 51 | 75 | 388 |
| **DIETARY FIBRE (g)** | 1 | 3 | 2 | 2 | 2 | 6 | 3 | 3 | 4 | 4 | 4 | 1 | 1 | 3 | 2 | 4 | 2 | 2 | 5 |
| **CARBOHYDRATE (g)** | 1 | 3 | 1 | 1 | 0 | 2 | 2 | 8 | 0 | 2 | 3 | 2 | 4 | 5 | 2 | 5 | 2 | 4 | 16 |
| **VITAMIN C (mg)** | 16 | 7 | 46 | 15 | 9 | 41 | 21 | 6 | 110 | 110 | 45 | 90 | 170 | 6 | 70 | 13 | 5 | 14 | 6 |
| **CALCIUM (mg)** | 30 | 20 | 70 | 11 | 20 | 17 | 42 | 8 | 31 | 15 | 35 | 8 | 2 | 34 | 14 | 41 | 36 | 17 | 22 |
| **SODIUM (mg)** | 6 | 5 | 13 | 2 | 2 | 4 | 3 | 54 | 21 | 30 | 18 | 2 | 1 | 45 | 15 | 21 | 88 | 8 | 3 |
| **VITAMIN A (ug)** | 15 | 3 | 230 | 8 | 49 | 34 | 61 | 3 | 65 | 28 | 6 | 31 | 250 | 1700 | 2 | 3 | 7 | 8 | 43 |
| **POTASSIUM (mg)** | 360 | 520 | 340 | 320 | 470 | 250 | 200 | 290 | 360 | 380 | 330 | 130 | 180 | 250 | 340 | 440 | 250 | 88 | 530 |
| **IRON (mg)** | 1 | 1 | 2 | 1 | 1 | 2 | 1 | 1 | 1 | 1 | 1 | 1 | 1 | 0 | 0 | 1 | 0 | 0 | 2 |

**Source:** Recommended Dietary Intakes for Use in Australia, *National Health & Medical Research Council, Australian Government Publishing Service, Canberra, 1991.* There is no RDI for dietary fibre. However, dietitians recommend an intake of 30g per day for adults.

| Recommended daily intakes: | Dietary fibre (g) | Carbohydrate (g) | Vitamin C (mg) | Calcium (mg) | Sodium (mg) | Vitamin A (ug) | Potassium (mg) | Iron (mg) |
|---|---|---|---|---|---|---|---|---|
| Men 19-64 yrs | 30 | 400 | 40 | 800 | 920-2300 | 750 | 1950-5460 | 7 |
| Women 19-54 yrs | 30 | 300 | 30 | 800 | 920-2300 | 750 | 1950-5460 | 12-16 |

| | Fennel | Kohlrabi | Kumara | Lettuce, cos | Lettuce, iceberg | Mushroom | Okra | Onion | Parsnip | Pea, green | Pea, sugar snap/snow | Potato | Pumpkin | Radish, red | Silverbeet | Spinach, English | Squash | Swede | Tomato | Turnip | Witlof | Zucchini |
|---|---|---|---|---|---|---|---|---|---|---|---|---|---|---|---|---|---|---|---|---|---|---|
| | 78 | 137 | 273 | 65 | 27 | 98 | 84 | 103 | 208 | 249 | 136 | 273 | 158 | 53 | 50 | 63 | 100 | 76 | 56 | 81 | 41 | 56 |
| | 3 | 3 | 2 | 2 | 2 | 3 | 4 | 2 | 3 | 6 | 2 | 2 | 1 | 1 | 3 | 3 | 2 | 3 | 1 | 3 | 2 | 2 |
| | 3 | 4 | 14 | 2 | 0 | 2 | 1 | 4 | 10 | 8 | 5 | 13 | 6 | 2 | 1 | 1 | 3 | 4 | 2 | 3 | 0 | 2 |
| | 9 | 71 | 31 | 13 | 4 | 1 | 34 | 7 | 12 | 32 | 46 | 23 | 16 | 23 | 21 | 27 | 26 | 27 | 18 | 23 | 18 | 24 |
| | 20 | 25 | 27 | 20 | 16 | 2 | 82 | 18 | 38 | 31 | 25 | 4 | 29 | 25 | 72 | 53 | 9 | 22 | 8 | 21 | 46 | 19 |
| | 38 | 16 | 10 | 18 | 23 | 7 | 2 | 13 | 19 | 2 | 1 | 3 | 1 | 20 | 195 | 21 | 3 | 12 | 6 | 24 | 76 | 1 |
| | 0 | 5 | 1130 | 100 | 15 | 5 | 20 | 2 | 5 | 71 | 33 | 0 | 500 | 3 | 195 | 390 | 55 | 0 | 58 | 0 | 73 | 63 |
| | 280 | 510 | 250 | 210 | 230 | 305 | 280 | 139 | 420 | 250 | 420 | 450 | 345 | 180 | 260 | 570 | 148 | 310 | 200 | 320 | 190 | 150 |
| | 0 | 1 | 1 | 1 | 1 | 0 | 1 | 0 | 0 | 2 | 1 | 1 | 1 | 1 | 2 | 3 | 0 | 0 | 0 | 0 | 2 | 1 |

# Artichokes

*An edible bud of a thistle-like member of the daisy family, the globe artichoke comes to us from North Africa. The Jerusalem artichoke, however, is neither from Jerusalem nor even an artichoke but a crisp tuber tasting a bit like water chestnut and named after the Italian word for sunflower, girasole.*

## Globe Artichokes

**COOKING METHODS** *Cooking times are based on 5 medium (1kg) globe artichokes, bases trimmed to sit flat, tough outer leaves discarded, rinsed under cold water.*

**BOIL** *Add globe artichokes to large pan of boiling water; boil, uncovered, about 30 minutes or until artichoke hearts are tender when pierced with a fork. Drain upside down; remove hairy choke with a spoon and discard it.*

**STEAM** *Place globe artichokes in single layer in steamer basket; cook, covered, over pan of simmering water about 40 minutes or until tender. Drain upside down; remove hairy choke with a spoon and discard it.*

**MICROWAVE** *Place globe artichokes and 1/4 cup (60ml) water in large microwave-safe dish. Cover, microwave on HIGH (100%) 15 minutes, pausing halfway during cooking time to turn. Drain upside down; remove hairy choke with a spoon and discard it.*
Tested in an 850-watt oven

### ARTICHOKE, PROSCIUTTO AND TOMATO BRAISE

**4 medium (800g) globe artichokes**
**2 tablespoons lemon juice**
**16 slices (240g) prosciutto**
**2 tablespoons olive oil**
**1 large (200g) onion, chopped**
**1 tablespoon chopped fresh oregano**
**1 tablespoon tomato paste**
**425g can tomatoes, undrained, crushed**
**1/2 cup (125ml) dry white wine**
**1 teaspoon chicken stock powder**

Boil, steam or microwave artichokes until just tender; drain. Quarter artichokes, remove and discard choke; brush artichoke pieces with juice. Wrap 1 slice prosciutto around each artichoke piece, secure with toothpick.

Heat oil in large pan; cook artichoke bundles, in batches, until prosciutto is browned all over. Remove from pan; remove and discard toothpicks. Cook onion in same pan, stirring, until soft. Add remaining ingredients; simmer, covered, about 10 minutes or until sauce thickens slightly. Add artichokes; simmer, covered, about 10 minutes or until heated through and tender.

Serves 4 to 6.

■ Best made just before serving.
■ Freeze: Not suitable.

### ARTICHOKE AND BROAD BEAN SALAD

**4 medium (800g) globe artichokes**
**1/4 cup (60ml) lemon juice**
**1/2 cup (125ml) olive oil**
**1 teaspoon sugar**
**1 clove garlic, crushed**
**1/3 cup chopped fresh mint leaves**
**500g packet frozen broad beans, cooked, peeled**
**1 1/3 cups (200g) kalamata olives**

Boil, steam or microwave artichokes until just tender; drain. Quarter artichokes; remove and discard choke.

Combine juice, oil, sugar, garlic and mint in jar; shake well. Toss warm artichokes, beans and olives with dressing in large bowl. Cover; refrigerate 3 hours or overnight.

Serves 4 to 6.

■ Best made a day ahead.
■ Storage: Covered, in refrigerator.
■ Freeze: Not suitable.

*Globe Artichokes*

*OPPOSITE FROM TOP: Artichoke and Broad Bean Salad; Artichoke, Prosciutto and Tomato Braise.*

# Artichokes

## ARTICHOKES ALLA ROMANA WITH BASIL MAYONNAISE

**4 medium (800g) globe artichokes**
**2 teaspoons olive oil**
**1 medium (350g) leek, sliced**
**1 small fresh red chilli,**
  **finely chopped**
**6 slices (200g) mortadella, chopped**
**¼ cup chopped fresh basil leaves**
**2 tablespoons chopped fresh parsley**
**3 cups (210g) stale breadcrumbs**
**½ cup (40g) grated parmesan cheese**

BASIL MAYONNAISE
**3 egg yolks**
**1 teaspoon seeded mustard**
**10 fresh basil leaves**
**1 clove garlic, crushed**
**1 tablespoon lemon juice**
**½ cup (125ml) olive oil**

Boil, steam or microwave artichokes until just tender; drain. Remove and discard inner leaves and hairy choke.

Heat oil in large pan; cook leek, chilli and mortadella, stirring, until leek is soft and mortadella almost crisp. Remove from heat; stir in herbs, breadcrumbs and cheese. Press breadcrumb seasoning between leaves and in centre of each artichoke. Wrap bottom half of each artichoke in foil, leaving seasoning uncovered; place artichokes in single layer in baking dish. Bake, uncovered, in moderate oven about 30 minutes or until tender and just browned. Just before serving, drizzle with Basil Mayonnaise.

**Basil Mayonnaise:** Blend or process egg yolks, mustard, basil, garlic and juice until smooth. With motor operating, gradually pour in oil; process until thick.

Serves 4.

■ Artichokes can be seasoned 3 hours ahead. Mayonnaise can be made a day ahead.
■ Storage: Covered, separately, in refrigerator.
■ Freeze: Not suitable.

*Plate from Grace Bros; jug from Wednesdays Value Homeware*

*LEFT: Artichokes alla Romana with Basil Mayonnaise.*
*OPPOSITE FROM TOP: Spanish-Style Jerusalem Artichoke Salad; Roasted Jerusalem Artichokes with Garlic; Char-Grilled Jerusalem Artichoke Salad.*

# Jerusalem Artichokes

**COOKING METHODS** *Steaming works best for this root vegetable. Peel 1kg small Jerusalem artichokes; cook, covered, in a steamer basket over a pan of simmering water about 20 minutes or until just tender. Drain.*

## ROASTED JERUSALEM ARTICHOKES WITH GARLIC

¼ cup (60ml) olive oil
15 large (1.5kg) Jerusalem artichokes
8 (200g) baby onions, quartered
1 medium bulb (70g) garlic, separated, unpeeled
2 sprigs fresh rosemary
¼ cup (60ml) balsamic vinegar
2 tablespoons brown sugar

Heat oil in large flameproof baking dish; cook artichokes, onions and garlic, stirring, until onions are soft. Add remaining ingredients; cook, stirring, until sugar dissolves. Transfer dish to moderately hot oven; bake, uncovered, about 1 hour or until artichokes are tender, stirring occasionally.

Serves 4 to 6.

■ Best made just before serving.
■ Freeze: Not suitable.
■ Microwave: Not suitable.

## CHAR-GRILLED JERUSALEM ARTICHOKE SALAD

12 medium (750g) Jerusalem artichokes, thinly sliced
2 tablespoons olive oil
2 medium (800g) kumara, thinly sliced
2 medium (400g) yellow capsicums
2 medium (400g) red capsicums

CHILLI MINT DRESSING
1½ cups firmly packed fresh mint leaves
½ cup (125ml) cider vinegar
½ cup (125ml) olive oil
¼ cup (60ml) sweet chilli sauce

Combine artichokes and oil in medium bowl; mix well.

Griddle-fry or barbecue artichoke and kumara slices, both sides, until just tender. Quarter capsicums, discard seeds and membranes; grill or barbecue capsicum pieces until skin blisters and blackens, peel away skin.

Gently toss vegetables with Chilli Mint Dressing in large bowl.

**Chilli Mint Dressing:** Blend or process all ingredients until smooth.

Serves 4 to 6.

■ Can be made 3 hours ahead.
■ Storage: Covered, in refrigerator.
■ Freeze: Not suitable.
■ Microwave: Not suitable.

## SPANISH-STYLE JERUSALEM ARTICHOKE SALAD

12 medium (750g) Jerusalem artichokes
2 medium (380g) tomatoes
120g rocket, trimmed
1 small (100g) red onion, sliced
1 cup (160g) black olives

SAFFRON PAPRIKA DRESSING
⅓ cup (80ml) white vinegar
½ cup (125ml) olive oil
1 clove garlic, crushed
¼ teaspoon saffron threads
¼ teaspoon sweet paprika
1 teaspoon sugar

Steam artichokes until just tender. Cut tomatoes into wedges. Gently toss artichokes, tomatoes and remaining ingredients with Saffron Paprika Dressing in large bowl.

**Saffron Paprika Dressing:** Combine all ingredients in jar; shake well.

Serves 4 to 6.

■ Salad best made just before serving. Saffron Paprika Dressing can be made a day ahead.
■ Storage: Covered, in refrigerator.
■ Freeze: Not suitable.

*Jerusalem Artichokes*

# Asian Vegetables

*Today's obsession with all manner of Asian cuisines naturally extends to a fascination with the beautifully unusual greens that so excited us in marketplaces from Bombay to Beijing... so much so, in fact, that now we treat them with scrupulous familiarity in our own kitchens.*

## Tat Soi and Mustard Greens

**COOKING METHODS** *Cooking times are based on 300g tat soi or 500g mustard greens, bases trimmed, leaves separated.*

**BOIL** *Add tat soi or mustard greens to large pan of boiling water; boil, uncovered, about 3 minutes or until tender. Drain.*

**STEAM** *Place tat soi or mustard greens in steamer basket; cook, covered, over pan of simmering water about 5 minutes or until tender. Drain.*

**MICROWAVE** *Place tat soi or mustard greens and 1 tablespoon water in large microwave-safe dish. Cover, microwave on HIGH (100%) about 3 minutes or until tender, pausing halfway during cooking time to stir. Drain.*

Tested in an 830-watt oven

### TAT SOI AND MUSTARD GREENS WITH PLUM SAUCE

1 tablespoon peanut oil
4 cloves garlic, sliced
2 tablespoons finely sliced
   fresh ginger
450g tat soi
500g mustard greens
1 tablespoon cornflour
1/4 cup (60ml) plum sauce
1 tablespoon soy sauce
1 tablespoon hoisin sauce

Heat oil in wok or large pan; stir-fry garlic and ginger until fragrant. Add tat soi and mustard greens then blended cornflour and sauces; stir until sauce boils and thickens.

Serves 4 to 6.

■ Best made just before serving.
■ Freeze: Not suitable.
■ Microwave: Not suitable.

*China from Waterford Wedgwood; tiles from Country Floors*

*Mustard Greens*

*Tat Soi*

8

# Asian Vegetables

## Choy Sum

*Choy Sum*

*Chinese Broccoli*

**COOKING METHODS** *Cooking times are based on 1kg choy sum, ends trimmed, open flowers removed and discarded.*

**BOIL** *Add choy sum to large pan of boiling water; boil, uncovered, about 4 minutes or until tender. Drain.*

**STEAM** *Place choy sum in steamer basket; cook, covered, over pan of simmering water about 4 minutes or until tender. Drain.*

**MICROWAVE** *Place choy sum and 1 tablespoon water in large microwave-safe dish. Cover, microwave on HIGH (100%) about 3 minutes or until tender, pausing halfway during cooking time to stir. Drain.*

Tested in an 830-watt oven

### CHOY SUM IN LIME AND COCONUT

**2 teaspoons cornflour**
**1 teaspoon sugar**
**2 tablespoons lime juice**
**1 teaspoon fish sauce**
**2/3 cup (160ml) coconut milk**
**1kg choy sum**

Blend cornflour and sugar with juice in wok or large pan; stir in sauce and milk. Stir until mixture boils and thickens. Add choy sum; stir until just wilted.

Serves 4.

■ Best made just before serving.
■ Freeze: Not suitable.
■ Microwave: Not suitable.

*ABOVE FROM LEFT: Choy Sum in Lime and Coconut; Hunan Vegetable Stir-Fry.*
*OPPOSITE: Chinese Zucchini Omelette.*

10

# Chinese Broccoli

**COOKING METHODS** *Cooking times are based on 900g Chinese broccoli, trimmed, chopped.*

**BOIL** *Add Chinese broccoli to large pan of boiling water; boil, uncovered, about 3 minutes or until tender. Drain.*

**STEAM** *Place Chinese broccoli in steamer basket; cook, covered, over pan of simmering water about 4 minutes or until tender. Drain.*

**MICROWAVE** *Place Chinese broccoli and 1 tablespoon water in large microwave-safe dish. Cover, microwave on HIGH (100%) about 3 minutes or until tender, pausing halfway during cooking time to stir. Drain.*
Tested in an 830-watt oven

## HUNAN VEGETABLE STIR-FRY

2 teaspoons cornflour
1/4 cup (60ml) lime juice
2 tablespoons peanut oil
2 tablespoons sweet chilli sauce
1 tablespoon fish sauce
900g Chinese broccoli
230g can water chestnuts, drained, sliced
250g mung bean sprouts, trimmed
1/3 cup (50g) unsalted peanuts, toasted, chopped

Blend cornflour with juice in wok or large pan; stir in oil and sauces. Stir until mixture boils and thickens. Add remaining ingredients; stir-fry about 3 minutes or until broccoli is just tender.

Serves 4 to 6.

■ Best made just before serving.
■ Freeze: Not suitable.
■ Microwave: Not suitable.

# Chinese Zucchini

**COOKING METHODS** *Cooking times are based on 1 medium (1kg) Chinese zucchini, fuzz removed with a damp cloth, cut as required.*

**BOIL** *Add Chinese zucchini to large pan of boiling water; boil, uncovered, about 6 minutes or until tender. Drain.*

**STEAM** *Place Chinese zucchini in steamer basket; cook, covered, over pan of simmering water about 7 minutes or until just tender. Drain.*

**MICROWAVE** *Place Chinese zucchini and 1 tablespoon water in large microwave-safe dish. Cover, microwave on HIGH (100%) about 5 minutes or until tender, pausing halfway during cooking time to stir. Drain.*
Tested in an 830-watt oven

## CHINESE ZUCCHINI OMELETTE

1 medium (1kg) Chinese zucchini
1 tablespoon peanut oil
1 small (200g) leek, finely chopped
2 cloves garlic, crushed
1 medium (200g) red capsicum, seeded, finely chopped
2 bacon rashers, finely chopped
8 eggs, lightly beaten
1/2 cup (60g) grated cheddar cheese

Slice zucchini in half lengthways, remove and discard seeds; grate zucchini coarsely.

Heat oil in deep 30cm pan; cook leek, garlic, capsicum and bacon, stirring, until capsicum is tender. Add eggs and half the cheese; cook over low heat until omelette has nearly set. Sprinkle top with remaining cheese; place omelette under heated grill about 2 minutes or until top is browned.

Serves 6.

■ Best made just before serving.
■ Freeze: Not suitable.
■ Microwave: Not suitable.

Chinese Zucchini

Plate from Accoutrement

# Asian Vegetables

*Bok Choy*

*Wing Beans*

## Wing Beans

**COOKING METHODS** *Cooking times are based on 500g wing beans, trimmed.*

**BOIL** *Add beans to large pan of boiling water; boil, uncovered, about 2 minutes or until tender. Drain.*

**STEAM** *Place beans in steamer basket; cook, covered, over pan of simmering water about 2 minutes or until tender. Drain.*

**MICROWAVE** *Place beans and 1 tablespoon water in large microwave-safe dish. Cover, microwave on HIGH (100%) about 4 minutes or until tender, pausing halfway during cooking time to stir. Drain.*

Tested in an 830-watt oven

## Bok Choy

**COOKING METHODS** *Cooking times are based on 800g baby bok choy, bases trimmed, leaves separated.*

**BOIL** *Add bok choy to large pan of boiling water; boil, uncovered, about 2 minutes or until tender. Drain.*

**STEAM** *Place bok choy in steamer basket; cook, covered, over pan of simmering water, about 3 minutes or until tender. Drain.*

**MICROWAVE** *Place bok choy and 1 tablespoon water in large microwave-safe dish. Cover, microwave on HIGH (100%) about 3 minutes or until tender, pausing halfway during cooking time to stir. Drain.*

Tested in an 830-watt oven

### SESAME BOK CHOY

**2 teaspoons cornflour**
**2 tablespoons water**
**2 tablespoons hoisin sauce**
**1 tablespoon oyster sauce**
**2 teaspoons soy sauce**
**2 teaspoons sesame oil**
**800g baby bok choy**
**1 tablespoon sesame seeds, toasted**

Blend cornflour with water in small jug; stir in sauces.

Heat oil in wok or large pan; stir-fry bok choy and seeds until bok choy is just tender. Stir in sauce mixture; stir until mixture boils and thickens.

Serves 4.

■ Best made just before serving.
■ Freeze: Not suitable.
■ Microwave: Suitable.

### WING BEANS IN PEANUT SAUCE

**500g wing beans**
**1/3 cup (85g) crunchy peanut butter**
**2 tablespoons sweet chilli sauce**
**1 tablespoon lemon juice**
**2/3 cup (160ml) chicken stock**
**2 teaspoons brown sugar**
**2 tablespoons coconut milk**

Boil, steam or microwave beans until just tender; drain.

Combine remaining ingredients in wok or large pan; simmer about 5 minutes or until mixture thickens slightly. Add beans; stir-fry until hot.

Serves 4 to 6.

■ Best made just before serving.
■ Freeze: Suitable.

# Chinese Water Spinach

**COOKING METHODS** *Cooking times are based on 175g Chinese water spinach, bases trimmed, leaves separated.*

**BOIL** *Add Chinese water spinach to large pan of boiling water; boil, uncovered, about 2 minutes or until tender. Drain.*

**STEAM** *Place Chinese water spinach in steamer basket; cook, covered, over pan of simmering water, about 3 minutes or until tender. Drain.*

**MICROWAVE** *Place Chinese water spinach and 1 tablespoon water in large microwave-safe dish. Cover, microwave on HIGH (100%) about 3 minutes or until tender, pausing halfway during cooking time to stir. Drain.*

Tested in an 830-watt oven

## CHINESE WATER SPINACH WITH CRISPY NOODLES

**360g Chinese water spinach**
**2 celery sticks, finely sliced**
**250g cherry tomatoes, halved**
**6 green onions, finely sliced**
**100g packet fried noodles**
**1/3 cup (35g) pecans, toasted, sliced**

SOY AND CHILLI DRESSING
**1/4 cup (60ml) peanut oil**
**2 tablespoons white vinegar**
**2 tablespoons sweet chilli sauce**
**1 tablespoon soy sauce**
**1/2 teaspoon sesame oil**

Combine all ingredients in large bowl with Soy and Chilli Dressing; toss gently.
**Soy and Chilli Dressing:** Combine all ingredients in jar; shake well.

Serves 6.

- Soy and Chilli Dressing can be made 3 days ahead. Recipe must be made just before serving.
- Storage: Dressing, covered, in refrigerator.
- Freeze: Not suitable.

*Chinese Water Spinach*

OPPOSITE: Sesame Bok Choy.
ABOVE LEFT: Chinese Water Spinach with Crispy Noodles.
LEFT: Wing Beans in Peanut Sauce.

# Asparagus

*Since there are few vegetables better than elegant fresh asparagus, it's one of life's great mysteries why so many people either overcook or ignore this tender young shoot belonging to the lily family. Whether you choose to cook the green or white variety, a handy rule of thumb to remember when judging readiness is that the tip droops slightly and the stem offers just the slightest resistance.*

**COOKING METHODS** *Cooking times are based on 500g asparagus, woody ends snapped off, lower part of stem peeled (from spear downward) with vegetable peeler if stems are thick.*

**BOIL** *Add asparagus to large pan of boiling water; boil, uncovered, about 3 minutes or until tender. Drain.*

**STEAM** *Place asparagus in steamer basket; cook, covered, over pan of simmering water about 4 minutes or until just tender. Drain.*

**MICROWAVE** *Place asparagus and 2 tablespoons water in large microwave-safe dish. Cover, microwave on HIGH (100%) about 3 minutes or until tender. Drain.*

Tested in an 830-watt oven

## ASPARAGUS SALAD WITH LEMON HERB VINAIGRETTE

**2 teaspoons olive oil**
**100g shaved smoked ham, chopped**
**1kg asparagus**
**50g firm brie cheese, chopped**
**1 medium (190g) tomato, seeded, chopped**

LEMON HERB VINAIGRETTE
**1 tablespoon red wine vinegar**
**2 tablespoons lemon juice**
**1/3 cup (80ml) light olive oil**
**1 tablespoon chopped fresh chives**
**1 tablespoon chopped fresh parsley**

Heat oil in small pan; cook ham, stirring, until browned and crisp. Cool.

Boil, steam or microwave asparagus until just tender. Drain then transfer to large bowl. Pour about three-quarters of Lemon Herb Vinaigrette over asparagus; gently toss to combine. Place asparagus on serving plate; scatter with ham, brie and tomato. Drizzle with remaining Lemon Herb Vinaigrette then serve immediately.

**Lemon Herb Vinaigrette:** Combine all ingredients in jar; shake well.

Serves 6 to 8.

- Best made just before serving. Lemon Herb Vinaigrette can be made 3 days ahead.
- Storage: Covered, in refrigerator.
- Freeze: Not suitable.

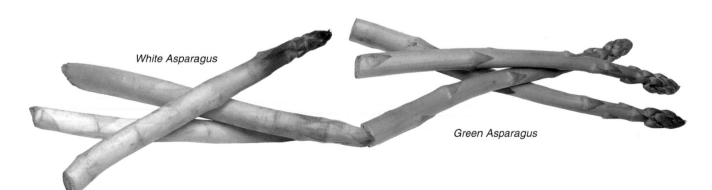

*White Asparagus*

*Green Asparagus*

# Asparagus

China from Accoutrement; napkin and spoon from Home & Garden on the Mall

## ASPARAGUS WITH THREE SAVOURY BUTTERS

*Asparagus is best cooked just before serving. Each of the butter recipes makes enough for 750g asparagus, which serves 6. Savoury butters can be made 3 days ahead and stored covered, separately, in refrigerator or frozen for up to 2 months.*

**750g asparagus**

Boil, steam or microwave asparagus until just tender; drain then transfer asparagus to large bowl. Add desired flavoured butter; gently toss asparagus to coat in butter as it melts.

## LEMON MUSTARD BUTTER

**80g butter, softened**
**1 tablespoon seeded mustard**
**1 tablespoon lemon juice**
**¼ teaspoon freshly cracked
    black pepper**

Combine all ingredients in small bowl; mix well.

## SUN-DRIED TOMATO BUTTER

**2 teaspoons olive oil**
**½ small (50g) red onion,
    finely chopped**
**2 teaspoons lemon juice**
**80g butter, softened**
**2 tablespoons chopped drained
    sun-dried tomatoes in oil**
**1 tablespoon chopped fresh parsley**

Heat oil in small pan; cook onion, stirring, until soft and fragrant. Cool. Combine onion with remaining ingredients in small bowl; mix well.

## HONEY NUT BUTTER

**80g butter, softened**
**1 tablespoon chopped fresh
    coriander leaves**
**1 tablespoon honey**
**2 tablespoons chopped macadamia
    nuts, toasted**
**1 teaspoon mild curry powder**
**½ teaspoon ground cumin**

Combine all ingredients in small bowl; mix well.

## ASPARAGUS AND ROCKET STIR-FRY

**750g asparagus**
**2 tablespoons olive oil**
**2 cloves garlic, crushed**
**1 medium (200g) red capsicum,
    seeded, sliced**
**2 tablespoons balsamic vinegar**
**2 tablespoons tomato paste**
**1 tablespoon water**
**125g rocket**

Cut each asparagus spear into 3 pieces. Heat oil in wok or large pan; stir-fry asparagus, garlic and capsicum until almost tender. Add combined vinegar, paste and water; stir-fry until asparagus is just tender. Add rocket; stir until just wilted.

Serves 4 to 6.

■ Best made just before serving.
■ Freeze: Not suitable.
■ Microwave: Not suitable.

*CLOCKWISE FROM TOP RIGHT:
Sun-Dried Tomato Butter; Lemon Mustard
Butter; Honey Nut Butter.
OPPOSITE: Asparagus and Rocket Stir-Fry.*

*Wurtz: A rather uncommon variety similar to the Fuerte but larger and more lemony with a freckled, lighter-green, smooth skin.*

*Hass: A definite pear-shape but an extremely thick neck. Deep purple to black bumpy skin; coarse yellow flesh and small seed. Slightly nutty, almost sweet flavour.*

*Sharwill: Ovoid in shape with a puckered, true-avocado coloured skin and citrus-yellow flesh. Smoky, full flavour; luscious spreadable texture.*

*Fuerte: Biggest of the avocados; olive-green, leathery skin and classic pear appearance. Skin separates easily from the pale flesh. Creamy, buttery and slightly nutty taste. Good mashed, especially in guacamole.*

# Avocados

*Vitamin-rich and cholesterol-free, the avocado is a nearly perfect food – how can it also taste as delicious as it does? One or more of the myriad varieties grown locally can be found year round, so the only limits to its use are those imposed by your imagination.*

## MEXICAN-STYLE BREAD SALAD

**2 large pieces pitta bread**
**1 tablespoon olive oil**
**2 medium (150g) egg tomatoes**
**2 large (640g) avocados, sliced**
**310g can corn kernels, rinsed, drained**
**300g can kidney beans, rinsed, drained**
**½ small cos lettuce**

GARLIC AND CHILLI DRESSING
**¼ cup (60ml) lemon juice**
**⅓ cup (80ml) olive oil**
**2 cloves garlic, crushed**
**1 teaspoon sambal oelek**
**2 tablespoons sweet chilli sauce**

Brush pitta both sides with oil, place on oven trays; bake in moderately hot oven about 15 minutes or until crisp. Cool; break into pieces.

Cut tomatoes in wedges; combine with avocados, corn and beans in large bowl. Just before serving, toss vegetable mixture with pitta pieces and Garlic and Chilli Dressing; place in lettuce-lined serving bowl.
**Garlic and Chilli Dressing:** Combine all ingredients in jar; shake well.

Serves 6.

- Pitta and Garlic and Chilli Dressing can be made a day ahead.
- Storage: Pitta, in airtight container. Dressing, covered, in refrigerator.
- Freeze: Not suitable.
- Microwave: Not suitable.

## SPINACH, PAWPAW AND AVOCADO SALAD

**1 bunch (500g) English spinach**
**¼ cup (40g) pine nuts, toasted**
**½ medium (500g) pawpaw, sliced**
**2 large (640g) avocados, sliced**

TANGY ORANGE DRESSING
**¼ cup (60ml) light olive oil**
**¼ cup (60ml) orange juice**
**1 teaspoon seeded mustard**
**2 teaspoons balsamic vinegar**

Combine all ingredients in large bowl; add Tangy Orange Dressing, mix gently.
**Tangy Orange Dressing:** Combine all ingredients in jar; shake well.

Serves 4.

- Must be made just before serving.
- Freeze: Not suitable.

## CREAMY AVOCADO AND MANGO SALAD

**1 cup (80g) mung bean sprouts**
**1/2 bunch (350g) watercress**
**1 medium (250g) avocado, sliced**
**2 sticks celery, sliced**
**1 medium (430g) mango, sliced**

CREAMY AVOCADO DRESSING
**1/2 small (100g) avocado**
**1/2 cup (125ml) buttermilk**
**1 teaspoon seeded mustard**
**1 tablespoon olive oil**
**1 tablespoon lemon juice**
**1 teaspoon wasabi paste**

Combine all ingredients in large bowl; drizzle with Creamy Avocado Dressing.
**Creamy Avocado Dressing**: Blend or process all ingredients until smooth.
Serves 4.

■ Must be made just before serving.
■ Freeze: Not suitable.

*OPPOSITE: Mexican-Style Bread Salad.*
*ABOVE FROM TOP: Creamy Avocado and Mango Salad; Spinach, Pawpaw and Avocado Salad.*

# Avocado Tips

■ Avocados are ripe if, when cradled in the palm of your hand, they yield to slight pressure. Don't prod an avocado with a finger unless you want to pierce the skin!

■ Black spots that appear in the flesh are caused by storage at cold temperatures: ripen avocados at room temperature if possible. They can be refrigerated for a maximum of 2 days in the least cold part of your refrigerator to slow the ripening process but any longer could cause them damage.

■ To hasten the ripening of avocados, seal them, along with a piece of apple, in a brown paper bag and leave in a warm corner of your kitchen.

■ When storing half a ripe avocado, leave the seed in and sprinkle with fresh lemon juice before covering.

# Beans

*Broad, round or flat; shelled or left podded; green, yellow or spotted – fresh beans of all descriptions are members of the same family, the legumes; dried, they are called pulses. Both ways, they constitute an internationally delicious force in both simple and more elegant cuisines.*

## Broad Beans

**COOKING METHODS** *Cooking times are based on 1kg broad beans, removed from outer pods.*

**BOIL** *Add broad beans to large pan of boiling water; boil, uncovered, 2 minutes. Drain then refresh under cold water; drain again.*

**STEAM** *Place broad beans in steamer basket; cook, covered, over pan of simmering water, 5 minutes. Drain then refresh under cold water; drain again.*

**MICROWAVE** *Place broad beans and 1/4 cup (60ml) water in large microwave-safe bowl. Cover, microwave on HIGH (100%) about 6 minutes or until tender, pausing halfway during cooking time to stir. Drain then refresh under cold water; drain again.*
Tested in an 830-watt oven

### CHILLI BEANS WITH TOMATOES, OLIVES AND FETTA

**1.5kg broad beans, shelled**
**1 tablespoon olive oil**
**1 small (100g) red onion, thinly sliced**
**1 clove garlic, crushed**
**1 small fresh red chilli, chopped**
**3 medium (570g) tomatoes, peeled, seeded, chopped**
**1/2 cup (125ml) dry white wine**
**2 tablespoons tomato paste**
**1/3 cup (50g) kalamata olives**
**2 teaspoons balsamic vinegar**
**2 teaspoons lemon juice**
**2 teaspoons sugar**
**250g fetta cheese, chopped**
**2 tablespoons chopped fresh flat-leaf parsley**

Boil, steam or microwave beans until tender. Drain; refresh under cold water, then remove and discard outer skins.

Heat oil in medium pan; cook onion, garlic and chilli, stirring, until onion is soft. Add tomatoes, wine, paste, olives, vinegar, juice and sugar; simmer, uncovered, about 8 minutes or until thickened. Gently stir in beans, fetta and half the parsley. Just before serving, sprinkle with remaining parsley.

Serves 4 to 6.

■ Best made on day of serving.
■ Freeze: Not suitable.

### BROAD BEAN AND POTATO GRATIN

**1kg broad beans, shelled**
**5 medium (1kg) potatoes**
**30g butter**
**2 tablespoons plain flour**
**2 cups (500ml) milk**
**2 teaspoons chicken stock powder**
**1 clove garlic, crushed**
**1/3 cup (40g) grated cheddar cheese**
**2 teaspoons chopped fresh thyme**
**1 tablespoon grated parmesan cheese**

Boil, steam or microwave beans until tender. Drain; refresh under cold water, then remove and discard outer skins. Cut potatoes into 2cm pieces; cook in large pan of boiling water, uncovered, until just tender. Drain.

Melt butter in small pan; add flour, stir over heat until bubbling. Remove from heat; gradually stir in milk until mixture boils and thickens. Stir in stock powder, garlic, cheddar and half the thyme; cook 1 minute.

Combine beans and potatoes in a shallow 1.5-litre (6-cup) ovenproof dish; pour sauce over vegetables. Scatter combined parmesan and remaining thyme over top; bake, uncovered, in moderate oven about 35 minutes or until browned lightly.

Serves 6.

■ Best made on day of serving.
■ Freeze: Not suitable.

*OPPOSITE FROM TOP:*
*Broad Bean and Potato Gratin;*
*Chilli Beans with Tomatoes, Olives and Fetta.*

Broad Beans

# Snake Beans

**COOKING METHODS** *Cooking times are based on 2 bunches (500g) snake beans, cut into 10cm lengths.*

**BOIL** *Add snake beans to large pan of boiling water; boil, uncovered, about 5 minutes or until tender. Drain.*

**STEAM** *Place snake beans in steamer basket; cook, covered, over pan of simmering water about 5 minutes or until tender. Drain.*

**MICROWAVE** *Place snake beans and 1 tablespoon water in large microwave-safe dish. Cover, microwave on HIGH (100%) about 5 minutes or until tender, pausing halfway during cooking time to stir. Stand 1 minute before serving. Drain.*
Tested in an 850-watt oven

## SNAKE BEAN, HAZELNUT AND ROASTED CAPSICUM SALAD

**2 bunches (500g) snake beans**
**2 large (700g) red capsicums, quartered, roasted**
**1/2 cup (75g) hazelnuts, toasted, roughly chopped**
**1/4 cup (60ml) orange juice**
**1/4 cup (60ml) olive oil**
**1 tablespoon white wine vinegar**
**1 teaspoon grated orange rind**
**1 teaspoon sugar**
**1/4 teaspoon cracked black pepper**
**1/4 teaspoon salt**

Cut beans into 8cm lengths. Boil, steam or microwave until just tender; drain. Slice capsicum pieces thinly. Gently toss beans, capsicum and nuts with combined remaining ingredients in medium bowl.

Serves 6.

■ Best made just before serving.
■ Freeze: Not suitable.

## CORIANDER PESTO SNAKE BEANS

**2 bunches (500g) snake beans**
**3 medium (225g) egg tomatoes, seeded, finely chopped**
**1 tablespoon pine nuts, toasted**
**1/4 cup (20g) parmesan cheese flakes**

CORIANDER PESTO
**110g fresh coriander leaves**
**2 tablespoons pine nuts, toasted**
**1 clove garlic, chopped**
**1/4 cup (20g) grated parmesan cheese**
**1/4 cup (60ml) olive oil**

Cut beans into 5cm lengths. Boil, steam or microwave until just tender; drain.

Gently toss beans, tomatoes, nuts and half the parmesan with Coriander Pesto in medium bowl. Just before serving, sprinkle with remaining parmesan.

**Coriander Pesto:** Remove and discard roots from coriander. Blend or process coriander, nuts, garlic and parmesan until almost smooth. With motor operating, gradually pour in oil; process until smooth.

Serves 6.

■ Best made just before serving. Coriander Pesto can be made a day ahead.
■ Storage: Covered, in refrigerator.
■ Freeze: Not suitable.

*Snake Beans*

# Green Beans

## COOKING METHODS
*Cooking times are based on 500g green beans, trimmed as desired.*

**BOIL** *Add green beans to large pan of boiling water; boil, uncovered, about 5 minutes or until tender. Drain.*

**STEAM** *Place green beans in steamer basket; cook, covered, over pan of simmering water about 6 minutes or until tender. Drain.*

**MICROWAVE** *Place green beans and 2 tablespoons water in microwave-safe dish. Cover, microwave on HIGH (100%) about 4 minutes or until tender, pausing halfway during cooking time to stir. Stand 1 minute before serving. Drain.*
Tested in an 850-watt oven

## ROMAN-STYLE GREEN BEANS
**3 slices (45g) prosciutto**
**500g green beans**
**2 tablespoons olive oil**
**200g button mushrooms**
**2 tablespoons pine nuts, toasted**
**1 tablespoon lemon juice**
**6 sprigs fresh lemon thyme**

Place prosciutto under hot grill until crisp; drain on absorbent paper. Snap prosciutto into small pieces; reserve. Trim stem ends of beans only.

Heat oil in wok or large pan; stir-fry mushrooms 1 minute. Add beans; stir-fry about 3 minutes or until just tender. Add prosciutto, nuts, juice and thyme; toss mixture gently until heated through.

Serves 4 to 6.
■ Best made just before serving.
■ Freeze: Not suitable.
■ Microwave: Not suitable.

*Bowls and platter from Home & Garden on the Mall; napkins and salad servers from The Bay Tree Kitchen Shop*

Green (French) Beans

*ABOVE*
*FROM TOP:*
*Coriander Pesto*
*Snake Beans;*
*Snake Bean,*
*Hazelnut and Roasted*
*Capsicum Salad.*
*RIGHT: Roman-Style Green Beans.*

# Beans

### CHAR-GRILLED POTATO, BEAN AND OLIVE SALAD

**500g butter beans, trimmed**
**500g tiny new potatoes, halved**
**1½ tablespoons olive oil**
**½ cup (80g) black olives**
**⅓ cup roughly chopped**
**fresh mint leaves**

SWEET CHILLI DRESSING
**2 tablespoons lemon juice**
**2 tablespoons olive oil**
**2 tablespoons sweet chilli sauce**

Boil, steam or microwave beans and potatoes, separately, until just tender; drain. Rinse beans under cold water; drain. Brush potatoes with oil; cook on heated oiled griddle pan or barbecue, cut-side down, until browned lightly and just tender. Gently mix beans, potatoes, olives and mint with Sweet Chilli Dressing in large bowl.
**Sweet Chilli Dressing:** Combine all ingredients in jar; shake well.

Serves 6.

■ Best made just before serving. Sweet Chilli Dressing can be made a day ahead.
■ Storage: Covered, in refrigerator.
■ Freeze: Not suitable.

### MIDDLE-EASTERN BEAN SALAD

**250g butter beans**
**250g green beans**
**3 teaspoons sumac [see Glossary]**
**1 small (100g) red onion,**
**finely chopped**
**⅓ cup roughly chopped fresh**
**flat-leaf parsley**
**¼ cup (60ml) lemon juice**
**2 tablespoons olive oil**
**1 tablespoon honey**
**1 clove garlic, crushed**

Boil, steam or microwave beans until almost tender. Rinse under cold water; drain. Gently mix beans with sumac, onion, parsley and combined remaining ingredients in large bowl.

Serves 6.

■ Best made just before serving.
■ Freeze: Not suitable.

## Butter Beans

**COOKING METHODS** *Cooking times are based on 500g butter beans, trimmed.*

**BOIL** *Add beans to large pan of boiling water; boil, uncovered, about 5 minutes or until tender. Drain.*

**STEAM** *Place beans in steamer basket; cook, covered, over pan of simmering water about 6 minutes or until tender. Drain.*

**MICROWAVE** *Place beans and 2 tablespoons water in large microwave-safe dish. Cover, microwave on HIGH (100%) about 4 minutes or until tender, pausing halfway during cooking time to stir. Stand 1 minute before serving. Drain.*

Tested in an 850-watt oven

### PAPRIKA TOMATO BEANS

**500g butter beans, trimmed**
**1 tablespoon olive oil**
**3 green onions, chopped**
**2 cloves garlic, crushed**
**1½ teaspoons sweet paprika**
**¼ cup (60ml) tomato puree**

Boil, steam or microwave beans until just tender; drain. Heat oil in large pan; cook onions and garlic 1 minute. Add paprika; cook 30 seconds. Stir in beans and puree until just heated through.

Serves 4 to 6.

■ Best made just before serving.
■ Freeze: Not suitable.

*Butter Beans*

*ABOVE LEFT: Paprika Tomato Beans.*
*OPPOSITE FROM TOP: Char-Grilled Potato, Bean and Olive Salad; Middle-Eastern Bean Salad.*

# Beans

# Borlotti Beans

## COOKING METHODS
*Cooking times are based on 1kg of borlotti beans, shelled.*

**BOIL** *Add borlotti beans to large pan of boiling water; boil, uncovered, about 20 minutes or until tender. Drain.*

**STEAM** *Place borlotti beans in steamer basket; cook, covered, over pan of simmering water about 30 minutes or until tender. Drain.*

**MICROWAVE** *Place borlotti beans and 2 tablespoons water in large microwave safe dish. Cover, microwave on HIGH (100%) about 15 minutes or until tender, pausing halfway during cooking time to stir. Stand 1 minute before serving. Drain.*
Tested in an 850-watt oven

*Borlotti Beans*

## BACON AND BEAN CASSEROLE
1 tablespoon vegetable oil
2 large (400g) onions, chopped
4 bacon rashers, chopped
2 x 425g cans tomatoes, undrained, crushed
1 cup (250ml) water
1 teaspoon chicken stock powder
1/4 cup (60ml) Worcestershire sauce
2 teaspoons Dijon mustard
1kg borlotti beans, shelled

Heat oil in large heavy-based pan; cook onions and bacon, stirring, until both are browned lightly. Add remaining ingredients; bring to boil, simmer, covered, about 1 hour or until beans are tender, stirring occasionally.

Serves 6 to 8.

■ Can be made a day ahead.
■ Storage: Covered, in refrigerator.
■ Freeze: Suitable.
■ Microwave: Suitable.

## BORLOTTI AND RED LENTIL DHAL
2 tablespoons ghee
1 tablespoon black mustard seeds
1/2 teaspoon black onion seeds (kalonji)
3 teaspoons cumin seeds
10 curry leaves, torn
2 medium (300g) onions, chopped
3 cloves garlic, crushed
1 tablespoon grated fresh ginger
1 small fresh red chilli, seeded, chopped
1 tablespoon ground coriander
1 teaspoon ground turmeric
2 x 400g can tomatoes, undrained, crushed
2 1/2 cups (625ml) vegetable stock
1 cup (200g) red lentils, rinsed
1kg borlotti beans, shelled
1/3 cup (80ml) cream
1/4 cup chopped fresh coriander leaves

Heat ghee in large heavy-based pan; cook seeds and curry leaves, stirring, until fragrant. Add onions, garlic, ginger and chilli; cook, stirring, until onions are soft. Stir in ground spices; cook, stirring, 1 minute. Add tomatoes, stock, lentils and beans; cook, covered, over low heat, about 1 hour or until beans are tender. Just before serving, stir in cream and half the coriander; when heated through, sprinkle with remaining coriander leaves.

Serves 6 to 8.

■ Can be prepared a day ahead.
■ Storage: Covered, in refrigerator.
■ Freeze: Suitable.
■ Microwave: Suitable.

bake, uncovered, in moderate oven, about 1 hour or until tomatoes are soft. Cover with foil if overbrowning.

Blend or process cooked vegetables with tomato paste and enough stock to make a smooth sauce.

Boil, steam or microwave beans until tender; drain. Place beans in serving bowl; spoon sauce over beans, sprinkle with parmesan and basil.

Serves 6 to 8.

■ Best made just before serving. Sauce can be made a day ahead; reheat before using.
■ Storage: Covered, in refrigerator.
■ Freeze: Not suitable.

## ITALIAN BEANS WITH RED CAPSICUM PESTO

**1kg Italian beans**

CAPSICUM PESTO
**2 large (700g) red capsicums, quartered, roasted**
**3/4 cup (60g) grated parmesan cheese**
**1 clove garlic, chopped**
**2/3 cup roughly chopped fresh basil leaves**
**1/4 cup (60ml) olive oil**

Boil, steam or microwave beans until tender; drain. Combine beans with capsicum pesto in large bowl; mix well.
**Capsicum Pesto:** Blend or process capsicums, cheese, garlic and basil until finely chopped. With motor operating, gradually pour in oil; process until combined.

Serves 6 to 8.

■ Best made just before serving. Capsicum Pesto can be made a day ahead.
■ Storage: Covered, in refrigerator.
■ Freeze: Not suitable.

# Italian Beans

### COOKING METHODS *Cooking times are based on 1kg Italian beans, halved.*

**BOIL** *Add Italian beans to large pan of boiling water; boil, uncovered, about 5 minutes or until tender. Drain.*

**STEAM** *Place Italian beans in steamer basket; cook, covered, over pan of simmering water about 5 minutes or until tender. Drain.*

**MICROWAVE** *Place Italian beans and 2 tablespoons water in large microwave-safe dish. Cover, microwave on HIGH (100%) about 5 minutes or until tender, pausing halfway through cooking time to stir. Stand 1 minute before serving. Drain.*

Tested in an 850-watt oven

## ITALIAN BEANS WITH TOMATO AND GARLIC SAUCE

**12 large (1kg) egg tomatoes**
**2 medium (300g) onions, quartered**
**8 cloves garlic, peeled**
**1/2 teaspoon sea salt**
**1/2 teaspoon cracked black pepper**
**2 tablespoons olive oil**
**1 1/2 tablespoons tomato paste**
**1/4 cup (60ml) vegetable stock, approximately**
**750g Italian beans, halved**
**1/4 cup (20g) parmesan cheese flakes**
**1/4 cup loosely packed fresh basil leaves, shredded**

Quarter tomatoes lengthways; place tomatoes, cut-side up, in large baking dish, with onions and garlic. Sprinkle with salt and pepper, drizzle with oil;

*Italian Beans*

*OPPOSITE TOP: Bacon and Bean Casserole.*
*OPPOSITE: Borlotti and Red Lentil Dhal.*
*ABOVE FROM TOP: Italian Beans with Red Capsicum Pesto; Italian Beans with Tomato and Garlic Sauce.*

# Beetroot

*Proof that opposites attract: the combination of a beetroot's outrageous colour and subtle sweet taste has resulted in the vegetable's astonishing popularity today, both in home and restaurant kitchens.*

**COOKING METHODS** *Cooking times are based on 3 medium (500g) beetroot, unpeeled, with 3cm of stem remaining.*

**BOIL** *Add beetroot to medium pan of boiling water; boil, uncovered, about 45 minutes or until tender. Drain; peel while still warm.*

**STEAM** *Place beetroot in steamer basket; cook, covered, over pan of simmering water about 55 minutes or until tender. Drain; peel while still warm.*

**MICROWAVE** *Place beetroot and 2 tablespoons water in large microwave-safe dish. Cover, microwave on HIGH (100%) about 30 minutes or until tender, pausing halfway during cooking time to turn. Drain; peel while still warm.*

Tested in an 830-watt oven

## BEETROOT AND POTATO MASH

**4 medium (650g) beetroot**
**3 medium (600g) potatoes**
**2 tablespoons cream**
**1/2 teaspoon sugar**
**50g butter**

Boil, steam or microwave beetroot and potatoes, separately, until tender; drain, peel while warm. Coarsely chop beetroot and potatoes; blend or process with remaining ingredients until pureed.

Serves 4 to 6.

■ Best made just before serving.
■ Freeze: Not suitable.

## BEETROOT SKEWERS

*You need 8 metal or sturdy bamboo skewers, each approximately 20 to 25cm in length, for this recipe. Buy similar-sized potatoes to make the finished dish look more attractive.*

**3 medium (500g) beetroot, peeled**
**4 tiny new potatoes, unpeeled, halved**
**2 small (160g) onions, quartered**
**1 tablespoon olive oil**
**2 tablespoons maple syrup**
**1/4 cup (60ml) cider vinegar**
**1 teaspoon grated orange rind**
**2 tablespoons orange juice**
**1 tablespoon chopped fresh mint leaves**

Quarter each beetroot; halve each quarter crossways. Thread 3 pieces of beetroot onto 1 skewer, separating with 1 piece each of potato and onion; brush skewered vegetables with oil. Place skewers in single layer in large baking dish; bake, uncovered, in moderate oven about 35 minutes or until vegetables are tender, turning twice during cooking.

Combine syrup, vinegar, rind and juice in small pan. Bring to boil; simmer, uncovered, about 5 minutes or until thickened slightly. Pour syrup mixture over skewers; sprinkle with mint.

Serves 4.

■ Best made just before serving.
■ Freeze: Not suitable.
■ Microwave: Not suitable.

*OPPOSITE FROM TOP: Beetroot and Potato Mash; Beetroot Skewers.*

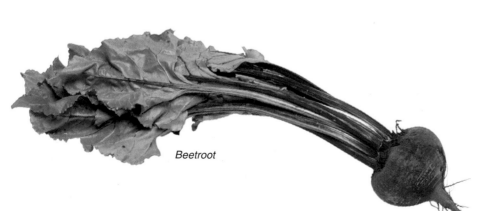
*Beetroot*

### RAW BEETROOT SALAD

*The easiest way to grate the beetroot
and onion is with a V-slicer [see
Glossary], but if you don't own one,
you can use a mandoline, the grating
disc on a food processor or the largest
holes of a hand grater.*

**4 medium (650g) beetroot, peeled
1 small (100g) red onion
2 tablespoons chopped fresh
    coriander leaves
¼ cup (60ml) olive oil
2 tablespoons lemon juice
1 teaspoon grated lemon rind
1 teaspoon sugar**

Grate beetroot and onion; toss with
coriander and combined remaining
ingredients in large bowl.

Serves 4 to 6.

■ Can be prepared 2 hours ahead.
■ Storage: Covered, in refrigerator.
■ Freeze: Not suitable.
■ Microwave: Not suitable.

### BABY BEETROOT SALAD WITH YOGURT MINT DRESSING

**2 bunches (1.2kg) baby beetroot
1 cup (250ml) yogurt
2 teaspoons honey
1 clove garlic, crushed
⅓ cup fresh mint leaves**

Boil, steam or microwave beetroot until
tender; drain, peel while warm. Blend
or process yogurt, honey, garlic and
mint until mint is finely chopped; pour
over beetroot to serve.

Serves 4 to 6.

■ Best made just before serving.
■ Freeze: Not suitable.

## BEETROOT MOUSSE

**4 to 5 large (1.5kg) beetroot,
 leaves intact**
**1 tablespoon gelatine**
**1 tablespoon water**
**½ cup (125ml) mayonnaise**
**½ cup (125ml) sour cream**
**¼ cup (60ml) sweet chilli sauce**
**1 teaspoon grated lemon rind**
**1 teaspoon salt**
**¼ cup (60ml) lemon juice**
**20g butter**

Cut through beetroot-leaf stems 3cm above beetroot; wash, trim, dry and reserve leaves.

Boil, steam or microwave beetroot until tender; drain. Peel while warm, chop coarsely (you should have approximately 3½ cups of chopped beetroot).

Sprinkle gelatine over water in cup placed in small pan of simmering water, stir until dissolved; cool slightly.

Blend or process beetroot, gelatine mixture, mayonnaise, cream, sauce, rind, salt and 1 tablespoon of the juice, in batches, until almost smooth. Pour mixture into oiled 22cm-round savarin pan; cover, refrigerate several hours or until firm.

Just before serving, heat butter in large pan; cook beetroot leaves, stirring, until just wilted. Stir in remaining lemon juice; cool. Turn mousse onto serving plate, fill centre with beetroot-leaf mixture.

Serves 6.

■ Beetroot-leaf mixture best made just before serving. Beetroot Mousse best made a day ahead.
■ Storage: Covered, in refrigerator.
■ Freeze: Not suitable.

*Fork from Cambur Industries*

*ABOVE FROM TOP LEFT:*
*Raw Beetroot Salad; Baby Beetroot Salad*
*with Yogurt Mint Dressing.*
*RIGHT: Beetroot Mousse.*

# Broccoli

*One maligned, the other virtually unknown, broccoli and broccoflower deserve better reputations. Excellent sources of Vitamin C, available all year, and edible raw or cooked, their respective flavours are distinctively delicious.*

## Broccoli

**COOKING METHODS** *Cooking times are based on 500g broccoli, cut into florets.*

**BOIL** *Add broccoli to medium pan of boiling water; boil, uncovered, about 3 minutes or until tender. Drain.*

**STEAM** *Place broccoli in single layer in steamer basket; cook, covered, over pan of simmering water about 7 minutes or until tender. Drain.*

**MICROWAVE** *Place broccoli and 1/4 cup (60ml) water in medium microwave-safe dish. Cover, microwave on HIGH (100%) about 5 minutes or until tender, pausing halfway during cooking time to stir. Drain.*

*Tested in an 850-watt oven*

### BROCCOLI WITH CHEESE AND BACON TOPPING

**750g broccoli**
**3 bacon rashers, chopped**
**40g butter**
**1/4 cup (35g) plain flour**
**1 teaspoon seeded mustard**
**1/3 cup (80ml) dry white wine**
**1 1/4 cups (310ml) milk**
**1/2 cup (60g) grated gruyere cheese**
**1/2 cup (60g) grated cheddar cheese**
**2 tablespoons grated parmesan cheese**

Boil, steam or microwave broccoli until just tender; drain. Cook bacon, stirring, in small dry pan until browned; drain on absorbent paper.

Melt butter in medium pan; add flour, stir over heat until bubbling. Remove from heat; gradually stir in mustard, wine and milk. Stir over heat until sauce boils and thickens; remove from heat, stir in cheeses.

Stand broccoli upright in shallow oiled 1.375-litre (5 1/2-cup) ovenproof dish; pour over cheese mixture, scatter bacon over top. Cook under hot grill about 5 minutes or until browned and heated through.

Serves 4 to 6.

■ Best made just before serving.
■ Freeze: Not suitable.
■ Microwave: Sauce suitable.

Broccoflower

Broccoli

# Broccoflower

**COOKING METHODS** *Cooking times are based on 500g broccoflower, cut into florets.*

**BOIL** *Add broccoflower to medium pan of boiling water; boil, uncovered, about 3 minutes or until tender. Drain.*

**STEAM** *Place broccoflower in single layer in steamer basket; cook, covered, over pan of simmering water about 4 minutes or until tender. Drain.*

**MICROWAVE** *Place broccoflower and ¼ cup (60ml) water in large microwave-safe dish. Cover, microwave on HIGH (100%) about 3 minutes or until tender, pausing halfway during cooking time to stir. Drain.*

Tested in an 850-watt oven

## BROCCOLI, BROCCOFLOWER AND CAULIFLOWER STIR-FRY

**2 tablespoons olive oil**
**1 medium (170g) red onion, cut into wedges**
**400g broccoli florets, sliced**
**400g broccoflower florets, sliced**
**400g cauliflower florets, sliced**
**¼ cup (60ml) cider vinegar**
**2 cloves garlic, crushed**
**1 tablespoon brown sugar**
**¼ cup chopped fresh basil leaves**

Heat oil in wok or large pan; cook onion, stirring, until soft. Add florets; cook, stirring, 2 minutes. Add combined remaining ingredients; cook, stirring gently, about 2 minutes or until florets are just tender.

Serves 4 to 6.

■ Best made just before serving.
■ Freeze: Not suitable.
■ Microwave: Not suitable.

## BROCCOFLOWER WITH BLUE CHEESE AND PECANS

**500g broccoflower florets**
**30g butter**
**1 medium (150g) onion, finely chopped**
**½ cup (125ml) dry white wine**
**½ cup (125ml) cream**
**125g creamy blue cheese, chopped**
**2 teaspoons cornflour**
**1 tablespoon water**
**2 tablespoons chopped pecans**

Boil, steam or microwave broccoflower until just tender; drain.

Heat butter in medium pan; cook onion, stirring, until soft. Add wine; simmer, uncovered, about 2 minutes or until wine reduces slightly. Add cream and cheese; stir over low heat until cheese melts. Add blended cornflour and water; cook, stirring, until sauce boils and thickens.

Place broccoflower in 1-litre (4-cup) ovenproof dish. Pour sauce over top, sprinkle with nuts. Bake, uncovered, in moderately hot oven about 15 minutes or until browned.

Serves 4.

■ Best made just before serving.
■ Freeze: Not suitable.
■ Microwave: Sauce suitable.

*OPPOSITE: Broccoli with Cheese and Bacon Topping.*
*ABOVE: Broccoli, Broccoflower and Cauliflower Stir-Fry.*
*BELOW: Broccoflower with Blue Cheese and Pecans.*

34

# Brussels Sprouts

*Members of the cabbage family, and resembling minuscule heads of cabbage too, Brussels sprouts were first cultivated in Belgium. Cultivate your taste for them by leaving in some of the crunch when cooking these nutty, sweet morsels.*

**COOKING METHODS** *Cooking times are based on 1kg Brussels sprouts.*

**BOIL** *Add Brussels sprouts to large pan of boiling water; boil, uncovered, about 8 minutes or until tender. Drain.*

**STEAM** *Place Brussels sprouts in single layer in steamer basket; cook, covered, over pan of simmering water about 10 minutes or until tender. Drain.*

**MICROWAVE** *Place Brussels sprouts and ¼ cup (60ml) water in large microwave-safe dish. Cover, microwave on HIGH (100%) about 8 minutes or until tender, pausing halfway during cooking time to stir. Drain.*

Tested in an 850-watt oven

## HONEY ORANGE BRUSSELS SPROUTS

**1kg Brussels sprouts**
**2 tablespoons orange juice**
**2 tablespoons seeded mustard**
**1 tablespoon honey**

Halve sprouts lengthways. Boil, steam or microwave until just tender; drain. Gently toss sprouts with combined remaining ingredients in serving bowl.

Serves 4 to 6.

■ Best made just before serving.
■ Freeze: Not suitable.

## BRUSSELS SPROUTS WITH BACON AND BREADCRUMBS

**1kg Brussels sprouts**
**100g butter**
**3 bacon rashers, chopped**
**2 cups (140g) stale breadcrumbs**
**4 green onions, chopped**
**1 tablespoon chopped fresh oregano**
**1 tablespoon chopped fresh basil leaves**
**1 tablespoon chopped fresh thyme**

Boil, steam or microwave sprouts until just tender; drain. Add about a third of the butter; mix well.

Heat remaining butter in large pan; cook bacon, stirring, until crisp. Add breadcrumbs; cook, stirring, until browned lightly. Add onions, herbs and sprouts; stir until heated through.

Serves 4 to 6.

■ Best made just before serving.
■ Freeze: Not suitable.

## BRUSSELS SPROUT AND CAPSICUM MELANGE

**1kg Brussels sprouts**
**2 tablespoons olive oil**
**2 medium (300g) onions, sliced**
**1 medium (200g) red capsicum, seeded, chopped**
**1 medium (200g) yellow capsicum, seeded, chopped**
**2 small fresh red chillies, chopped**
**50g butter**
**2 tablespoons brown sugar**
**⅓ cup (50g) pine nuts, toasted**

Boil, steam or microwave sprouts until just tender; drain.

Heat oil in large pan; cook onions, stirring, until soft. Add capsicums and chillies; cook, stirring, until soft. Add butter and sugar; cook, stirring, until sugar has dissolved. Add pine nuts and sprouts; stir until heated through.

Serves 4 to 6.

■ Best made just before serving.
■ Freeze: Not suitable.

*CLOCKWISE FROM TOP: Brussels Sprout and Capsicum Melange; Brussels Sprouts with Bacon and Breadcrumbs; Honey Orange Brussels Sprouts.*

*Brussels Sprouts*

# Cabbages

*Regardless of continent or culture, cabbage lifts its head in innumerable rustic soups, salads and casseroles. Traditionally a peasant food, grown in the harshest of climates and poorest of soils, it also has the capability of transforming itself, with the help of a keen cook, into many tasty dishes, good enough to set before a king.*

## SUMMERTIME CABBAGE SALAD

400g red cabbage, shredded
300g savoy cabbage, shredded
1 small (150g) red capsicum, seeded, sliced
1 small (150g) yellow capsicum, seeded, sliced
4 green onions, chopped
½ cup (80g) pine nuts, toasted

### TANGY HERB DRESSING
1 tablespoon tomato paste
1 tablespoon lemon juice
2 tablespoons balsamic vinegar
2 tablespoons water
⅓ cup (80ml) light olive oil
2 cloves garlic, crushed
2 tablespoons chopped fresh coriander leaves

Combine all ingredients in large bowl; toss gently with Tangy Herb Dressing.
**Tangy Herb Dressing:** Combine all ingredients in jar; shake well.

## COOKING METHODS
*Cooking times are based on 900g cabbage, coarsely chopped.*

**BOIL** *Add cabbage to large pan of boiling water; boil, uncovered, about 9 minutes or until tender. Drain.*

**STEAM** *Place cabbage in steamer basket; cook, covered, over pan of simmering water about 12 minutes or until tender. Drain.*

**MICROWAVE** *Place cabbage and 2 tablespoons water in large microwave-safe dish. Cover, microwave on HIGH (100%) about 9 minutes or until tender, pausing halfway during cooking time to stir. Drain.*

Tested in an 850-watt oven

Red Cabbage

Serves 6 to 8.

■ Summertime Cabbage Salad best assembled just before serving. Tangy Herb Dressing can be made a day ahead.
■ Storage: Covered, in refrigerator.
■ Freeze: Not suitable.

## BRAISED RED CABBAGE

**50g butter**
**900g red cabbage, chopped**
**2 teaspoons red wine vinegar**
**¼ cup (60ml) redcurrant jelly**

Heat butter in large pan. Add cabbage; cook, stirring, until just soft. Add vinegar and jelly; cook, stirring, about 2 minutes or until heated through.

Serves 6.

■ Best made just before serving.
■ Freeze: Not suitable.
■ Microwave: Suitable.

*Bowl and plate from Villeroy & Boch*

*Plates and bowl from Home & Garden on the Mall*

## WARM THAI-STYLE CABBAGE AND RICE SALAD

**1 cup (200g) white long-grain rice**
**2 cups (160g) broccoli florets**
**2 tablespoons peanut oil**
**900g Chinese cabbage, chopped**
**3 cloves garlic, crushed**
**2 teaspoons grated fresh ginger**
**3 teaspoons fish sauce**
**¼ cup (60ml) sweet chilli sauce**
**2 tablespoons lime juice**
**2 tablespoons chopped raw peanuts**
**2 tablespoons finely chopped fresh coriander leaves**

Cook rice in large pan of boiling water, uncovered, until just tender; drain. Rinse rice under cold water; drain.

Boil, steam or microwave broccoli until just tender; drain.

Heat oil in wok or large pan; stir-fry cabbage, garlic and ginger until cabbage is just soft. Add rice, broccoli and combined sauces, juice and peanuts; cook, stirring, until heated through. Just before serving, stir through coriander.

Serves 6.

■ Best made just before serving.
■ Freeze: Not suitable.
■ Microwave: Suitable.

*OPPOSITE FROM LEFT:*
*Summertime Cabbage Salad;*
*Warm Thai-Style Cabbage and Rice Salad.*
*ABOVE: Braised Red Cabbage.*

*Basket and pewter platter from Bayteak Leisure Store; black wok from Made on Earth*

## STIR-FRIED LEAFY CHINESE GREENS

**2 tablespoons peanut oil**
**900g Chinese cabbage, chopped**
**340g baby bok choy, chopped**
**4 green onions, chopped**
**1 tablespoon soy sauce**
**2 tablespoons oyster sauce**
**2 teaspoons sesame oil**
**1 teaspoon sesame seeds, toasted**

Heat peanut oil in wok or large pan; stir-fry cabbage until it begins to soften. Add bok choy, stirring, until just tender. Stir in onions, sauces and sesame oil; stir-fry until well combined and heated through. Serve sprinkled with sesame seeds.

Serves 4 to 6.

■ Best made just before serving.
■ Freeze: Not suitable.
■ Microwave: Not suitable.

## CREAMY SPICED CABBAGE

**2 tablespoons vegetable oil**
**1 small (80g) onion, sliced**
**3 cloves garlic, crushed**
**2 teaspoons grated fresh ginger**
**2 teaspoons finely chopped fresh lemon grass**
**1 large (200g) onion, sliced**
**900g savoy cabbage, chopped**
**1 tablespoon mild curry paste**
**2 teaspoons plain flour**
**270ml can coconut milk**
**1 tablespoon lime juice**
**2 teaspoons fish sauce**
**1/4 teaspoon black onion seeds (kalonji)**

Heat half the oil in small pan. Add small onion; cook until browned and crisp. Drain on absorbent paper; reserve.

Heat remaining oil in large pan; cook garlic, ginger, lemon grass and large onion, stirring, until onion is soft. Add cabbage; cook, stirring, about 10 minutes or until soft. Add curry paste and flour; cook, stirring, about 2 minutes or until well combined. Add milk, juice and sauce; simmer, uncovered, about 5 minutes or until mixture thickens slightly. Just before serving, top with reserved fried onion, sprinkle with onion seeds.

Serves 6.

■ Best made just before serving.
■ Freeze: Not suitable.
■ Microwave: Not suitable.

*Savoy Cabbage*

*Common Round Cabbage*

*Chinese Cabbage*

## CABBAGE ROLLS

*We used common round cabbage for this recipe.*

12 large cabbage leaves
2 cups (500ml) water
2 medium (380g) tomatoes, chopped
2 tablespoons tomato paste
1/4 cup (60ml) lemon juice
4 cloves garlic, crushed

RICE FILLING
1/2 cup (100g) uncooked white
    long-grain rice
200g minced lamb
1 tablespoon tomato paste
1 teaspoon salt

Remove and discard thick stems from leaves. Boil, steam or microwave leaves until just soft; drain. Rinse leaves under cold water; drain.

Place leaves, vein-side up, on work surface; divide filling among them, placing portion at stem end of each leaf. Roll up firmly, folding in sides to enclose filling. Place rolls close together, seam-side down, in large pan; pour over combined water, tomatoes and paste. Cover rolls with heatproof plate to keep in position during cooking. Bring to boil; simmer, covered, 25 minutes. Remove cover and plate; pour combined juice and garlic over rolls. Simmer, uncovered, about 10 minutes or until sauce thickens.

**Rice Filling:** Combine ingredients in medium bowl; mix thoroughly.

Makes 12.

■ Best made on day of serving.
■ Storage: Covered, in refrigerator.
■ Freeze: Not suitable.
■ Microwave: Suitable.

*Pointed Head Cabbage*

## COLESLAW WITH A TRIO OF DRESSINGS

*Each one of the three recipes on the right makes enough dressing for this amount of coleslaw.*

450g pointed head
    cabbage, shredded
1 large (180g) carrot,
    coarsely grated
1 medium (200g) red capsicum,
    seeded, sliced
3 green onions, chopped
1/4 cup chopped fresh
    flat-leaf parsley

Combine all ingredients in large bowl; gently toss with preferred dressing.

Serves 6.

■ Coleslaw best made just before serving. Dressings can be made a day ahead.
■ Storage: Covered, separately, in refrigerator.
■ Freeze: Not suitable.

## MAYONNAISE DRESSING

1/3 cup (80ml) mayonnaise
1/3 cup (80ml) sour cream
1/2 teaspoon sugar
1 teaspoon Dijon mustard
1 tablespoon boiling water
2 tablespoons lime juice

Combine all ingredients in jug or small bowl; mix well.

Makes about 1 cup (250ml).

## LOW-FAT DRESSING

1/3 cup (80ml) buttermilk
1/3 cup (80ml) low-fat yogurt
1 tablespoon water
2 tablespoons lemon juice

Combine all ingredients in jug or small bowl; mix well.

Makes about 1 cup (250ml).

## VINAIGRETTE

1/2 cup (125ml) olive oil
1/4 cup (60ml) white vinegar
2 tablespoons lemon juice
1 tablespoon seeded mustard
3 cloves garlic, crushed

Combine all ingredients in jar; shake well.

Makes about 1 cup (250ml).

*OPPOSITE FROM LEFT:*
*Stir-Fried Leafy Chinese Greens; Creamy Spiced Cabbage.*
*LEFT: Cabbage Rolls.*
*ABOVE, CLOCKWISE FROM TOP:*
*Vinaigrette; Mayonnaise Dressing;*
*Low-Fat Dressing; Coleslaw.*

*Glass bowl from Bayteak Leisure Store; wooden box and salad servers from Made on Earth*

*Yellow Capsicum*

*Green Capsicum*

*Red Capsicum*

*Purple Capsicum*

*RIGHT FROM TOP: Capsicum, Chickpea and Olive Salad; Roasted Capsicums with Port and Basil Dressing.*
*OPPOSITE: Grilled Capsicums with Rocket Pesto.*

## ROASTED CAPSICUMS WITH PORT AND BASIL DRESSING

**2 medium (400g) red capsicums**
**2 medium (400g) green capsicums**
**2 medium (400g) yellow capsicums**
**10 green onions**
**8 cloves garlic**
**4 small (400g) onions, quartered**
**1 tablespoon olive oil**

PORT AND BASIL DRESSING
**1/2 cup (125ml) olive oil**
**1/4 cup (60ml) balsamic vinegar**
**2 cloves garlic**
**1/3 cup firmly packed fresh basil leaves**
**1 tablespoon port**
**1 tablespoon mild chilli sauce**

Quarter capsicums; remove and discard seeds and membranes. Combine with remaining ingredients in large baking dish; bake, uncovered, in moderate oven 1 hour. Drizzle with Port and Basil Dressing while still warm.

**Port and Basil Dressing:** Blend or process all ingredients until pureed.

Serves 6 to 8.

■ Best made just before serving.
■ Freeze: Not suitable.
■ Microwave: Not suitable.

# Capsicums

*Columbus is responsible for the confusion over this food's name, erroneously naming it a pepper when he took it from the New World to Europe. It's really a large, mild member of the chilli family – but, by any other name, is just as delectably sweet.*

## CAPSICUM, CHICKPEA AND OLIVE SALAD

3/4 cup (150g) dried chickpeas
2 medium (400g) red capsicums, seeded, chopped
2 medium (400g) green capsicums, seeded, chopped
1 medium (170g) red onion, chopped
1/3 cup fresh flat-leaf parsley
3/4 cup (120g) black olives

LEMON DRESSING
1/3 cup (80ml) olive oil
1 medium (150g) onion, chopped
2 cloves garlic, crushed
2 teaspoons ground cumin
1 teaspoon hot paprika
1/4 cup (60ml) lemon juice

Cover chickpeas with cold water in medium bowl; stand overnight.

Drain chickpeas; rinse under cold water. Place chickpeas in large pan of boiling water; simmer, uncovered, about 45 minutes or until just tender. Drain; rinse under cold water until cool. Drain well then toss chickpeas with remaining ingredients and Lemon Dressing in large bowl.
**Lemon Dressing:** Heat 1 tablespoon of the oil in small pan; cook onion, garlic and spices, stirring, until onion is soft. Blend or process onion mixture with remaining oil and juice until smooth.

Serves 4 to 6.

■ Best made just before serving.
■ Freeze: Not suitable.
■ Microwave: Chickpeas suitable.

## GRILLED CAPSICUMS WITH ROCKET PESTO

3 medium (600g) red capsicums
3 medium (600g) yellow capsicums
1/3 cup (50g) roasted macadamias, chopped

ROCKET PESTO
60g rocket, trimmed
1/4 cup (20g) grated parmesan cheese
1 clove garlic
1/4 cup (35g) macadamias, toasted, roughly chopped
1/2 cup (125ml) olive oil

Quarter capsicums; remove and discard seeds and membranes. Roast under grill or in very hot oven, skin-side up, until skin blisters and blackens. Cover capsicum pieces in plastic or paper for 5 minutes; peel away skin. Slice pieces in half lengthways; gently toss with nuts and Rocket Pesto in serving bowl.
**Rocket Pesto:** Blend or process all ingredients until pureed.

Serves 4 to 6.

■ Best made just before serving.
■ Freeze: Not suitable.
■ Microwave: Not suitable.

*Plate from Villeroy & Boch*

# Carrots

*Crunching on a cold, crisp carrot is irresistibly satisfying, plus it's a bite full of fibre and betacarotene. A member of the parsley family, the carrot is multi-talented, as good in juices, cakes and dips as it is in soups and stews.*

**COOKING METHODS** *Cooking times are based on 3 large (540g) carrots, peeled, cut into 1cm slices.*

**BOIL** *Add carrots to large pan of boiling water; boil, uncovered, about 7 minutes or until tender. Drain.*

**STEAM** *Place carrots in steamer basket; cook, covered, over pan of simmering water about 9 minutes or until tender. Drain.*

**MICROWAVE** *Place carrots and 1/4 cup (60ml) water in large microwave-safe dish. Cover, microwave on HIGH (100%) about 8 minutes or until tender, pausing halfway during cooking time to stir. Drain.*
Tested in an 850-watt oven

## MINTED BABY CARROTS WITH GARLIC

**30g butter**
**2 cloves garlic, crushed**
**2 bunches (800g) baby carrots, trimmed**
**1/2 teaspoon sugar**
**1/4 cup (60ml) lemon juice**
**2 tablespoons chopped fresh mint leaves**

Heat butter in large shallow pan; cook garlic, stirring, about 2 minutes or until fragrant. Add carrots, sugar and juice; cook, stirring, about 8 minutes or until carrots are tender. Sprinkle with mint.

Serves 4 to 6.

■ Best made just before serving.
■ Freeze: Not suitable.
■ Microwave: Suitable.

## MOROCCAN CARROT SALAD

**3 large (540g) carrots, grated**
**1/2 cup (115g) chopped fresh seeded dates**
**1/2 cup (70g) slivered almonds, toasted**
**1/4 cup chopped fresh coriander leaves**
**1/4 cup (60ml) olive oil**
**1/4 cup (60ml) white vinegar**
**2 teaspoons ground cumin**
**1 tablespoon honey**

Combine carrots, dates, nuts and coriander in large bowl; gently toss with combined remaining ingredients.

Serves 4 to 6.

■ Can be made 1 hour ahead.
■ Storage: Covered, in refrigerator.
■ Freeze: Not suitable.

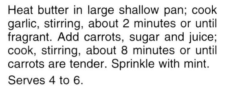

*Carrot*

*Baby or Dutch Carrots*

## CARROT QUENELLES

**4 large (700g) carrots, chopped**
**20g butter**
**1/3 cup (80ml) cream**
**pinch ground nutmeg**

Boil, steam or microwave carrots; drain. Blend or process carrots with remaining ingredients until pureed. Using two dessertspoons, form carrot mixture into oval-shaped quenelles.

Serves 4.

■ Best made just before serving.
■ Freeze: Not suitable.

*ABOVE LEFT: Moroccan Carrot Salad.*
*LEFT: Carrot Quenelles.*
*ABOVE: Minted Baby Carrots with Garlic.*

43

## HOT AND SWEET CAULIFLOWER

**2 tablespoons peanut oil**
**2 fresh long red chillies, chopped**
**2 cloves garlic, crushed**
**1 tablespoon finely chopped fresh lemon grass**
**500g cauliflower florets**
**¼ cup (60ml) water**
**1 teaspoon fish sauce**
**2 tablespoons sweet chilli sauce**
**2 green onions, chopped**

Heat oil in medium pan; cook chillies, garlic and lemon grass, stirring, about 2 minutes or until fragrant. Add cauliflower and water; cook, covered, about 5 minutes or until cauliflower is almost tender. Stir in sauces; cook, uncovered, until cauliflower is tender. Just before serving, stir in onions.

Serves 4.
■ Best made just before serving.
■ Freeze: Not suitable.
■ Microwave: Suitable.

## CURRIED CAULIFLOWER

**1 tablespoon ghee**
**1 medium (150g) onion, chopped**
**1 clove garlic, crushed**
**1 tablespoon grated fresh ginger**
**1 teaspoon cumin seeds**
**1 teaspoon mustard seeds**
**1 teaspoon ground cumin**
**1 teaspoon ground coriander**
**½ teaspoon ground turmeric**
**270ml can coconut milk**
**¼ cup (60ml) water**
**500g cauliflower florets**
**1 medium (190g) tomato, chopped**
**1 tablespoon chopped fresh coriander leaves**

Heat ghee in medium pan; cook onion, garlic and ginger, stirring, until onion is soft. Add seeds and spices; cook, stirring frequently, about 5 minutes or until fragrant. Stir in remaining ingredients; simmer, uncovered, about 10 minutes or until cauliflower is just tender and sauce thickened.

Serves 4 to 6.
■ Can be made 3 hours ahead.
■ Storage: Covered, in refrigerator.
■ Freeze: Not suitable.
■ Microwave: Suitable.

# Cauliflower

*Literally a cabbage cultivated for its tightly furled, edible white florets, cauliflower is another native of North Africa, introduced to the rest of the world by Arab traders. Its gentle, rather bland flavour is an adaptable foil for a great many different treatments.*

**COOKING METHODS** *Cooking times are based on 500g cauliflower, cut into florets.*

**BOIL** *Add cauliflower to large pan of boiling water; boil, uncovered, about 4 minutes or until tender. Drain.*

**STEAM** *Place cauliflower in steamer basket; cook, covered, over pan of simmering water about 4 minutes or until tender. Drain.*

**MICROWAVE** *Place cauliflower and 1/4 cup (60ml) water in large microwave-safe dish. Cover, microwave on HIGH (100%) about 6 minutes or until tender, pausing halfway during cooking time to stir. Stand 1 minute; drain.*

Tested in an 850-watt oven

## CAULIFLOWER GNOCCHI

**2 cups (500ml) milk**
**1/4 teaspoon chilli powder**
**1/2 cup (80g) semolina**
**400g cauliflower, chopped**
**1 teaspoon salt**
**3/4 cup (60g) grated**
  **parmesan cheese**
**1 egg, lightly beaten**
**20g butter, melted**
**1 tablespoon chopped fresh parsley**

Oil 26cm x 32cm Swiss roll pan.

Bring milk and chilli powder to boil in medium pan; gradually stir in semolina, cauliflower and salt. Simmer, uncovered, about 12 minutes or until mixture is very thick, stirring frequently. Combine 1/2 cup (40g) of the parmesan with egg; stir into cauliflower mixture. Spread gnocchi mixture into prepared pan; cover, refrigerate 3 hours or until firm.

Using a 4cm cutter, cut gnocchi mixture into rounds; using spatula, lift rounds onto baking paper-lined tray. Place leftover gnocchi scraps in oiled shallow ovenproof dish; top with overlapping gnocchi, brush with butter, sprinkle with remaining parmesan. Bake, uncovered, in moderate oven about 20 minutes or until gnocchi are browned and heated through. Sprinkle with parsley.

Serves 4.

- Cauliflower Gnocchi mixture can be prepared a day ahead.
- Storage: Covered, in refrigerator.
- Freeze: Not suitable.
- Microwave: Not suitable.

*Cauliflower*

*OPPOSITE FROM LEFT: Hot and Sweet Cauliflower; Curried Cauliflower.
RIGHT: Cauliflower Gnocchi.*

# Celeriac

*Sometimes called knob celery, celeriac is a round brown root having a delicious white flesh. The French have long appreciated its flavour but celeriac has only just become popular here, thanks to its frequent appearance on brasserie menus.*

**COOKING METHODS** *Cooking times are based on 1 large (1.25kg) celeriac, peeled, cut into 2cm pieces (approximately 7 cups).*

**BOIL** *Add celeriac to large pan of boiling water; boil, uncovered, about 30 minutes or until tender. Drain.*

**STEAM** *Place celeriac in steamer basket; cook, covered, over pan of simmering water about 40 minutes or until tender. Drain.*

**MICROWAVE** *Place celeriac and 1/4 cup (60ml) water in large microwave-safe dish. Cover, microwave on HIGH (100%) about 20 minutes or until tender, pausing halfway during cooking time to stir. Stand 2 minutes; drain.*

Tested in an 830-watt oven

## CELERIAC MASH

**1 large (1.25kg) celeriac**
**50g butter**
**1/3 cup (80ml) buttermilk**
**1/2 teaspoon ground nutmeg**
**4 green onions, chopped**

Boil, steam or microwave celeriac until tender; drain. Mash celeriac with butter, buttermilk and nutmeg in large bowl; stir in onions, and salt and pepper to taste.

Serves 4 to 6.

■ Best made just before serving.
■ Freeze: Not suitable.

## ROAST CELERIAC WITH GARLIC PARSLEY BUTTER

**1 large (1.25kg) celeriac, chopped into 5cm pieces**
**1 tablespoon olive oil**
**1 medium bulb (70g) garlic**
**50g butter**
**1/4 cup chopped fresh flat-leaf parsley**

Toss celeriac in oil; place with the unpeeled garlic in large flameproof baking dish. Bake, uncovered, in moderate oven about 1 hour or until celeriac is tender; remove from pan, keep warm. Cut whole garlic in half horizontally; squeeze pulp into baking dish, discard skin. Add butter and parsley; cook, stirring, until butter melts. Return celeriac to dish, toss gently with garlic mixture.

Serves 4 to 6.

■ Best made just before serving.
■ Freeze: Not suitable.
■ Microwave: Not suitable.

## CELERIAC SALAD WITH HORSERADISH MAYONNAISE

**1 medium (760g) raw celeriac, grated**
**1 large (200g) apple, grated**
**1 large (180g) carrot, grated**

HORSERADISH MAYONNAISE
**3 egg yolks**
**1 tablespoon white wine vinegar**
**1 tablespoon chopped fresh sage**
**2 teaspoons horseradish cream**
**1/2 cup (125ml) olive oil**

Combine salad ingredients in large bowl; add Horseradish Mayonnaise, toss gently.
**Horseradish Mayonnaise:** Blend or process egg yolks, vinegar, sage and horseradish cream until smooth. With motor operating, gradually pour in oil; process until thick.

Serves 4 to 6.

■ Can be prepared 3 hours ahead.
■ Storage: Covered, in refrigerator.
■ Freeze: Not suitable.

*Celeriac*

*CLOCKWISE FROM TOP LEFT: Celeriac Mash; Celeriac Salad with Horseradish Mayonnaise; Roast Celeriac with Garlic Parsley Butter.*

# Celery

*Too often relegated to the back-burner and used only as a base ingredient, celery stands out in the parsley family for its delicately distinct flavour and crisp texture.*

## GAZPACHO CELERY SALAD

*You need a large bunch (1.5kg) of celery for this recipe.*

**1/3 cup (65g) red lentils**
**1 small (125g) Lebanese cucumber**
**125g rocket**
**1 cup (100g) walnuts, toasted**
**10 (750g) sticks celery, trimmed, finely sliced**
**350g teardrop tomatoes, halved**

GAZPACHO DRESSING
**1/2 cup (125ml) tomato juice**
**1 tablespoon olive oil**
**1 tablespoon chopped fresh dill**
**1 clove garlic, crushed**
**1 teaspoon sugar**
**1 teaspoon red wine vinegar**
**1/2 teaspoon Tabasco sauce**

Rinse lentils under cold water; drain. Cook lentils in small pan of boiling water, uncovered, about 5 minutes or until just tender; drain, cool.

Halve cucumber lengthways then slice halves finely. Combine lentils and cucumber slices with remaining salad ingredients in large bowl; gently toss with Gazpacho Dressing.

**Gazpacho Dressing:** Combine all ingredients in jar; shake well.

Serves 6.

■ Salad best made just before serving. Dressing can be made a day ahead.
■ Storage: In jar, in refrigerator.
■ Freeze: Not suitable.

*Casserole dish from House*

## PROSCIUTTO AND TOMATO BAKED CELERY

*You need 2 large bunches (3kg) of celery for this recipe. Remove as much string from sticks of celery as possible.*

**20 (1.4kg) sticks celery**
**1 tablespoon olive oil**
**20g butter**
**1 medium (150g) onion, finely chopped**
**5 slices (75g) prosciutto, chopped**
**1 clove garlic, crushed**
**4 large (360g) egg tomatoes, chopped**
**1/3 cup (80ml) beef stock**
**1/3 cup (25g) grated parmesan cheese**

Cut celery into 10cm lengths. Cook in large pan of boiling water, covered, 6 minutes; drain. Heat oil and butter in large heavy-based pan; cook onion, prosciutto and garlic, stirring, until onion is soft. Add celery, tomatoes and stock; cook, covered, 20 minutes. Transfer mixture to shallow 3-litre (12-cup) ovenproof dish; sprinkle parmesan over the top. Bake, uncovered, in moderately hot oven, about 20 minutes or until browned lightly.

Serves 6 to 8.

■ Best made just before serving.
■ Freeze: Not suitable.
■ Microwave: Celery suitable.

*OPPOSITE: Gazpacho Celery Salad.*
*ABOVE: Prosciutto and Tomato Baked Celery.*

*Celery*

# Chokoes

*Known as chayote, christophene and vegetable pear in various parts of the world, this member of the squash family grows wild from the West Indies to Latin America, where it is regarded as a kitchen staple. The Mexicans, especially, eat it in numerous dishes – from a deep-fried snack with salsa to a dessert stewed with tropical fruits.*

Plates and cutlery from House In Newtown

**COOKING METHODS** *Cooking times are based on 3 large (1kg) chokoes, peeled, seeded and cut into 3cm wedges.*

**BOIL** *Add chokoes to large pan of boiling water; boil, uncovered, about 12 minutes or until tender. Drain.*

**STEAM** *Place chokoes, in single layer, in steamer basket; cook, covered, over pan of simmering water about 15 minutes or until tender. Drain.*

**MICROWAVE** *Place chokoes and 1/4 cup (60ml) water in large microwave-safe bowl. Cover, microwave on HIGH (100%) about 9 minutes or until tender, pausing halfway during cooking time to stir. Stand 2 minutes; drain.*

Tested in an 830-watt oven

*Choko*

## CHOKO AND POTATO PUREE

**2 teaspoons olive oil**
**1 large (500g) leek, finely chopped**
**1 clove garlic, crushed**
**3 large (1kg) chokoes, chopped**
**6 medium (1.2kg) potatoes, chopped**
**50g butter, chopped**
**2 teaspoons chicken stock powder**
**2 tablespoons chopped fresh basil leaves**

Heat oil in small pan; cook leek and garlic, stirring, about 5 minutes or until leek is soft.

Boil, steam or microwave chokoes and potatoes, separately, until tender; drain. Blend or process chokoes with the leek mixture until pureed; mash potatoes with butter and stock powder. Combine both mixtures; push through sieve into large bowl, stir through basil.

Serves 4 to 6.

■ Can be made 3 hours ahead.
■ Storage: Covered, in refrigerator.
■ Freeze: Not suitable.

## CRUMBED CHOKO WEDGES

**5 medium (875g) chokoes**
**1/2 cup (50g) packaged breadcrumbs**
**1/4 cup (20g) finely grated parmesan cheese**
**1 clove garlic, finely chopped**
**2 teaspoons chopped fresh thyme**
**1 egg, lightly beaten**
**vegetable oil, for shallow frying**

Cut each choko into 8 wedges. Boil, steam or microwave until just tender; drain, pat dry.

Combine breadcrumbs, parmesan, garlic and thyme in large bowl. Dip wedges in egg, then in breadcrumb mixture. Heat oil in large shallow pan; fry wedges, in batches, until well browned all over. Drain on absorbent paper.

Makes 40.

■ Best made just before serving.
■ Freeze: Not suitable.

## CREAMY BACON CHOKOES

**8 small (800g) chokoes**
**2 teaspoons olive oil**
**3 bacon rashers, finely chopped**
**2 medium (300g) onions, chopped**
**2 cloves garlic, crushed**
**1/3 cup (80ml) cream**
**2 teaspoons Dijon mustard**
**1 tablespoon chopped fresh parsley**

Quarter chokoes lengthways. Boil, steam or microwave until tender; drain.

Heat oil in large pan; cook bacon, onions and garlic, stirring, until onions are soft. Add chokoes and combined remaining ingredients to pan; stir gently until heated through.

Serves 4 to 6.

■ Best made just before serving.
■ Freeze: Not suitable.

*CLOCKWISE FROM TOP LEFT:*
*Choko and Potato Puree; Creamy Bacon Chokoes; Crumbed Choko Wedges.*

# Corn

Corn, native to the Americas, was introduced by the Indians to the early settlers – no wonder they said Thanks for the Giving. Also known as maize, corn is dried and ground into meal for polenta, into powder for flour or left intact to be popped: kernels of inspiration!

**COOKING METHODS** *Cooking times are based on 2 medium (600g) fresh corn cobs, husk and silk removed and discarded.*

**BOIL** *Add corn to medium pan of boiling water; boil, uncovered, about 10 minutes or until tender. Drain.*

**STEAM** *Place corn in steamer basket; cook, covered, over pan of simmering water, about 15 minutes or until tender. Drain.*

**MICROWAVE** *Place corn and 1 tablespoon water in medium microwave-safe dish. Cover, microwave on HIGH (100%) about 5 minutes or until tender, pausing halfway during cooking time to turn. Drain.*
Tested in an 850-watt oven

## CORN, BARLEY AND TOMATO SALAD

3 medium (900g) corn cobs
2/3 cup (130g) pearl barley, rinsed
2 large (700g) green capsicums, roasted, finely chopped
2 large (500g) tomatoes, seeded, sliced
1 medium (170g) red onion, thinly sliced
1 baby cos lettuce
1/3 cup chopped fresh mint leaves

SWEET CHILLI DRESSING
1/3 cup (80ml) olive oil
2 tablespoons sweet chilli sauce
2 tablespoons lemon juice
1 teaspoon sugar

Boil, steam or microwave corn until tender; drain. When cool, cut kernels from cobs in strips; discard cobs. Cook barley in medium pan of boiling water, uncovered, about 35 minutes or until tender; drain. Gently toss corn and barley with remaining salad ingredients and Sweet Chilli Dressing in large bowl.
**Sweet Chilli Dressing:** Combine all ingredients in jar; shake well.

Serves 6 to 8.

■ Sweet Chilli Dressing can be made a day ahead. Salad best made on day of serving.
■ Storage: Covered, separately, in refrigerator.
■ Freeze: Not suitable.

*Plate from Villeroy & Boch; tiles from Country Floors*

*Corn*

52

## BARBECUED CORN WITH LIME BUTTER

**6 small (1.5kg) corn cobs,
   husks intact**

LIME BUTTER
**125g butter, softened
2 teaspoons grated lime rind
1 small fresh red chilli,
   seeded, chopped
1 tablespoon chopped fresh
   coriander leaves**

Gently peel husk down corn cob, keeping husk attached at base. Remove as much silk as possible then bring husk back over cob to re-wrap and enclose completely; secure husk at end of cob with string. Cover corn cobs with cold water in large bowl, stand at least 1 hour; drain. Do not allow husk to dry; use as soon as possible after draining.

Cook corn on heated oiled barbecue or griddle pan about 25 minutes or until corn is just tender, turning occasionally. Discard string, serve immediately with Lime Butter.

**Lime Butter:** Combine all ingredients in small bowl; spoon mixture onto piece of plastic wrap, shape into a 12cm log. Roll up; refrigerate until firm.

Makes 6.

- Corn can be soaked up to 8 hours before cooking. Lime Butter can be made a week ahead.
- Storage: Butter, covered, in refrigerator.
- Freeze: Butter suitable.

## SUCCOTASH

*You need approximately 2 medium (600g) corn cobs for this recipe. Remove kernels by running a sharp knife down sides of each cob.*

**50g butter
1 small (80g) onion, finely chopped
1 bacon rasher, finely chopped
2 cups (330g) fresh corn kernels
2 small (300g) red capsicums,
   finely chopped
500g packet frozen broad beans,
   cooked, peeled
1/4 cup (60ml) cream**

Heat butter in large pan; cook onion, bacon, corn and capsicums, stirring, about 5 minutes or until corn is tender. Add remaining ingredients, stir until heated through.

Serves 6.

- Best made on day of serving.
- Storage: Covered, in refrigerator.
- Freeze: Not suitable.
- Microwave: Not suitable.

*OPPOSITE: Corn, Barley and Tomato Salad.
RIGHT FROM TOP: Barbecued Corn with
Lime Butter; Succotash.*

## INDONESIAN CUCUMBER SALAD WITH PEANUT DRESSING

**2 medium (240g) carrots**
**1 (400g) telegraph cucumber, sliced**
**3 cups (240g) mung bean sprouts**
**1 tablespoon chopped fresh**
   **coriander leaves**

PEANUT DRESSING
**1/3 cup (85g) smooth peanut butter**
**1 clove garlic, crushed**
**1 teaspoon sambal oelek**
**1 tablespoon soy sauce**
**1/2 cup (125ml) coconut milk**
**2 tablespoons hot water**

Using a vegetable peeler, cut carrots into long thin strips. Gently toss carrot with remaining salad ingredients in large bowl; drizzle with Peanut Dressing.
**Peanut Dressing:** Combine peanut butter, garlic, sambal oelek, sauce and milk in small bowl. Just before serving, stir in hot water.

Serves 4 to 6.

■ Salad and Peanut Dressing can be prepared 3 hours ahead.
■ Storage: Covered, separately, in refrigerator.
■ Freeze: Not suitable.

## LAYERED CUCUMBER SALAD

**2 large (180g) egg tomatoes**
**1 (250g) apple cucumber, peeled**
**1 small (100g) red onion,**
   **cut into rings**

HERB DRESSING
**1/4 cup (60ml) olive oil**
**1 tablespoon balsamic vinegar**
**2 teaspoons chopped**
   **fresh marjoram**
**1/2 teaspoon sugar**

Cut tomatoes into 5mm slices; slice cucumber into 5mm rounds. Layer the tomatoes, cucumber and onion in medium bowl; drizzle with Herb Dressing. Cover; refrigerate at least 1 hour before serving.
**Herb Dressing:** Whisk all ingredients in small jug until combined.

Serves 4.

■ Salad and Herb Dressing can be prepared 3 hours ahead.
■ Storage: Covered, separately, in refrigerator.
■ Freeze: Not suitable.

*LEFT FROM TOP: Indonesian Cucumber Salad with Peanut Dressing;*
*Layered Cucumber Salad;*
*Cucumber and Daikon Salad.*
*OPPOSITE: Sweet Chilli Cucumber Salad.*

Bowl and placemats from Home & Garden on the Mall

Raffia mat from Orson & Blake Collectables

Place setting from Made in Japan

# Cucumbers

*Thin-skinned yet cool, the multi-talented cucumber can be pungent in a pickle or soothingly sweet in a salad.*

## SWEET CHILLI CUCUMBER SALAD

**5 medium (650g) Lebanese cucumbers**
**2/3 cup (100g) raw peanuts, toasted**
**4 green onions, chopped**
**2 tablespoons chopped fresh coriander leaves**
**1 tablespoon lime juice**

SWEET CHILLI DRESSING
**1 cup (250ml) white vinegar**
**1/2 cup (125ml) sweet chilli sauce**
**1 tablespoon fish sauce**
**1 tablespoon sugar**
**1 clove garlic, crushed**

Halve cucumbers lengthways; discard seeds, cut diagonally into 1cm slices. Just before serving, gently toss the cucumber, remaining salad ingredients and Sweet Chilli Dressing together in medium bowl.
**Sweet Chilli Dressing:** Combine all ingredients in small pan; boil, uncovered, about 10 minutes or until reduced to 3/4 cup (180ml). Cool.

Serves 4.

■ Sweet Chilli Dressing can be made a day ahead.
■ Storage: Covered, in refrigerator.
■ Freeze: Not suitable.

## CUCUMBER AND DAIKON SALAD

**3 medium (390g) Lebanese cucumbers**
**1/2 (390g) daikon [see Radish]**
**1/4 cup (40g) drained pickled pink ginger**
**2 green onions, chopped**

WASABI DRESSING
**3/4 teaspoon wasabi paste**
**2 tablespoons peanut oil**
**1 tablespoon rice vinegar**

Using a vegetable peeler, cut cucumbers and daikon into long thin strips. Gently toss cucumber and daikon strips with remaining salad ingredients in large bowl; drizzle with Wasabi Dressing.
**Wasabi Dressing:** Whisk all ingredients in small jug until combined.

Serves 4 to 6.

■ Best made just before serving.
■ Freeze: Not suitable.

*Placemat and glass bowl from Home & Garden on the Mall*

*Telegraph Cucumber: An old variety dating back to the days when the telegraph was a new invention. Very long and green with ridges running down its entire length; also called a Continental Cucumber.*

*Apple Cucumber: Short, round, plump and pale green in colour. Very fleshy, loaded with soft seeds; its sweet flavour and juiciness make it quite popular.*

*Green Cucumber: This long, oval-shaped cucumber is the most common.*

*Lebanese Cucumber: Also known as the European or Burpless Cucumber, this variety is long, slender and dark green. It is favoured for its juiciness and digestibility.*

# Eggplants

*European folklore has it that eating eggplant skin caused insanity but we prefer the Turkish tale where the sultan fainted with pleasure upon eating a dish of tiny stuffed eggplants... proof of the allure of this seductive vegetable.*

## BOMBAY BABY EGGPLANTS

8 (480g) baby eggplants
2 tablespoons peanut oil
2 teaspoons grated fresh ginger
2 cloves garlic, crushed
1 small fresh red chilli,
   finely chopped
2 teaspoons ground cumin
2 teaspoons sesame seeds
2 teaspoons coriander seeds
1 teaspoon poppy seeds
3/4 cup (180ml) coconut milk
1 tablespoon tamarind pulp
2 tablespoons coconut milk, extra

Quarter eggplants lengthways but do not cut all the way through at stem end.

Heat oil in wok or large pan; stir-fry ginger, garlic, chilli, ground and whole spices 1 minute or until fragrant. Add eggplants; stir-fry 2 minutes. Add milk and tamarind; cook, covered, about 8 minutes or until eggplants are tender, stirring occasionally. Drizzle with extra coconut milk just before serving.

Serves 4 to 6.

■ Best made on day of serving.
■ Storage: Covered, in refrigerator.
■ Freeze: Not suitable.
■ Microwave: Not suitable.

## BABA GHANOUSH AND VEGETABLE JULIENNE

1 small (130g) Lebanese cucumber
1 medium (120g) green zucchini
1 medium (120g) yellow zucchini
1 medium (120g) carrot

BABA GHANOUSH DRESSING
2 (120g) baby eggplants
1 clove garlic, crushed
2 tablespoons tahini
1½ teaspoons ground cumin
½ cup (125ml) buttermilk
2 tablespoons water
2 tablespoons chopped fresh
   coriander leaves

Halve cucumber lengthways; discard seeds. Slice cucumber, zucchini and carrot into paper-thin 10cm strips; place in medium bowl, drizzle with Baba Ghanoush Dressing.

**Baba Ghanoush Dressing:** Pierce eggplants all over with fork, place on oven tray; bake, uncovered, in hot oven about 45 minutes or until flesh is soft and skin is blackened. Peel; discard skin, chop flesh roughly. Blend or process eggplant,

Plate from Villeroy & Boch

garlic, tahini and cumin until pureed. Add buttermilk and water; process until smooth. Stir in coriander.

Serves 6.
- ■ Baba Ghanoush Dressing can be made a day ahead.
- ■ Storage: Covered, in refrigerator.
- ■ Freeze: Not suitable.
- ■ Microwave: Not suitable.

## EGGPLANT SALAD CAPRESE

**3 small (690g) eggplants**
**salt**
**2 medium (380g) tomatoes, sliced**
**350g bocconcini cheese, sliced**
**¼ cup firmly packed**
**    fresh basil leaves**

CLASSIC ITALIAN DRESSING
**¼ cup (60ml) olive oil**
**1 clove garlic, crushed**
**1 teaspoon seeded mustard**
**1 teaspoon sugar**
**2 tablespoons red wine vinegar**

Cut eggplants into 1cm slices, place on wire racks, sprinkle with salt; stand 30 minutes. Rinse eggplant under cold water; drain on absorbent paper. Cook eggplant in heated oiled griddle pan until tender and browned on both sides.

Layer eggplant with remaining salad ingredients on serving platter; drizzle with three-quarters of the Classic Italian Dressing. Cover; refrigerate for at least 15 minutes or up to 3 hours. Just before serving, drizzle with the remaining Classic Italian Dressing.

**Classic Italian Dressing:** Combine all ingredients in a jar; shake well.

Serves 4 to 6.
- ■ Can be made up to 3 hours before serving.
- ■ Storage: Covered, in refrigerator.
- ■ Freeze: Not suitable.

*Eggplant*

*Baby Eggplant*

*OPPOSITE: Bombay Baby Eggplants.*
*RIGHT FROM TOP:*
*Baba Ghanoush and Vegetable Julienne;*
*Eggplant Salad Caprese.*

### FENNEL, ASPARAGUS AND ANCHOVY STIR-FRY

1 tablespoon olive oil
1 large (700g) fennel bulb, sliced
250g asparagus, chopped
½ small (75g) red capsicum,
    seeded, finely chopped
2 tablespoons lemon juice
60g butter
3 cloves garlic, crushed
4 anchovy fillets, finely chopped

Heat oil in wok or large pan; stir-fry fennel and asparagus 2 minutes. Add capsicum, juice and combined butter, garlic and anchovies; stir-fry until the vegetable are just tender.

Serves 4 to 6.

■ Best made just before serving.
■ Freeze: Not suitable.
■ Microwave: Not suitable.

### FENNEL AND TOMATO FRITTERS WITH YOGURT

1 small (450g) fennel bulb,
    finely chopped
2 large (500g) tomatoes,
    seeded, chopped
1 small (80g) onion, finely chopped
1 small fresh red chilli, seeded,
    finely chopped
2 teaspoons grated lemon rind
¼ cup (20g) grated parmesan cheese
1 cup (125g) grated cheddar cheese
1 cup (150g) plain flour
3 eggs, lightly beaten
vegetable oil, for deep-frying

YOGURT DIPPING SAUCE
200ml yogurt
1 tablespoon lemon juice
1 tablespoon water
2 teaspoons chopped fresh
    fennel leaves

Combine fennel, tomatoes, onion, chilli, rind, cheeses, flour and eggs in medium bowl. Just before serving, deep-fry rounded tablespoons of mixture in hot oil, in batches, until just browned; drain on absorbent paper. Serve warm with Yogurt Dipping Sauce.

**Yogurt Dipping Sauce:** Combine all ingredients in small bowl; mix well.

Makes about 20.

Serves 4 to 6.

■ Fritters best made just before
    serving. Yogurt Dipping Sauce can
    be made a day ahead.
■ Storage: Covered, in refrigerator.
■ Freeze: Not suitable.

# Fennel

*Often known by its Italian name of finocchio (and all too often wrongly called anise), fragrant fennel looks a bit like celery, tastes a bit like licorice and, braised with garlic, butter and parmesan, becomes a dish to die for.*

**COOKING METHODS** *Cooking times are based on 2 medium (1.2kg) fennel bulbs, stalks and leaves removed, halved lengthways, bases trimmed to separate halves.*

**BOIL** *Add fennel pieces to large pan of boiling water; cook, uncovered, about 5 minutes or until tender. Drain.*

**STEAM** *Place fennel in steamer basket; cook, covered, over pan of simmering water about 5 minutes or until tender. Drain.*

**MICROWAVE** *Place fennel and 1/4 cup (60ml) water in large microwave-safe bowl. Cover, microwave on HIGH (100%) about 5 minutes or until tender, pausing halfway during cooking time to turn. Drain.*

Tested in a 750-watt oven

*Fennel*

## FENNEL RIVIERA SALAD

1 large (700g) fennel bulb,
  thinly sliced
3 large (270g) egg tomatoes,
  halved, sliced
1 small (100g) red onion,
  thinly sliced
300g can chickpeas, rinsed, drained
1 cup (160g) black olives

BASIL VINAIGRETTE
1/4 cup (60ml) olive oil
2 tablespoons lemon juice
2 cloves garlic, crushed

2 tablespoons shredded fresh
  basil leaves
1 teaspoon ground cumin

Just before serving, gently toss all salad ingredients with Basil Vinaigrette in large bowl.
**Basil Vinaigrette**: Combine all ingredients in jar; shake well.
Serves 4.

■ Best made just before serving.
■ Freeze: Not suitable.

*OPPOSITE FROM TOP: Fennel, Asparagus and Anchovy Stir-Fry; Fennel and Tomato Fritters with Yogurt. ABOVE: Fennel Riviera Salad.*

# Jicama

*Think of the word hiccup, and you'll remember how to pronounce the name of the nutty, crunchy jicama (hik-kah-mah), similar to a fresh water chestnut but slightly sweeter in flavour. Looking like a misshapen brown beetroot, the jicama is also called a yam bean or Mexican potato and can be eaten cooked or raw.*

## JICAMA AND MANGO SALSA

1 medium (500g) jicama, peeled, chopped
2 large mangoes, chopped
1 teaspoon ground cumin
1 tablespoon chopped fresh coriander leaves
1/4 teaspoon hot chilli powder
2 tablespoons olive oil
2 tablespoons lime juice

Jicama

Boil, steam or microwave jicama until just tender; drain. Refresh under cold water; drain, pat dry with absorbent paper. Gently toss jicama and mango with combined remaining ingredients in medium bowl.

Serves 4 to 6.
■ Can be made 3 hours before serving.
■ Storage: Covered, in refrigerator.
■ Freeze: Not suitable.

*LEFT: Jicama and Mango Salsa.*
*ABOVE, CLOCKWISE FROM TOP RIGHT: Kohlrabi in Lemon, Cream and Dill Sauce; Kohlrabi Wedges with Salsa Fresca; Honey-Glazed Kohlrabi and Carrots.*

Kohlrabi

# Kohlrabi

*Kohlrabi, also known as cabbage turnip, is a purple-tinged, bulbous stem with dark-veined leaves sprouting out randomly over its surface. Rich in potassium, kohlrabi has a nutty, slightly turnip-like taste, and both stem and leaves are appetising additions to soups and stews. Eaten raw in salads, steamed or mashed, kohlrabi is in a delicious class of its own.*

**COOKING METHODS** *Cooking times are based on 3 medium (1.5kg) kohlrabi, leaves removed, peeled, chopped into 3cm pieces.*

**BOIL** *Add kohlrabi to large pan of boiling water; cook, uncovered, about 10 minutes or until tender. Drain.*

**STEAM** *Place kohlrabi, in single layer, in steamer basket; cook, covered, over pan of simmering water about 10 minutes or until tender. Drain.*

**MICROWAVE** *Place kohlrabi and 2 tablespoons water in large microwave-safe bowl. Cover, microwave on HIGH (100%) about 12 minutes or until tender, pausing halfway during cooking time to stir. Drain.*

Tested in a 750-watt oven

## KOHLRABI IN LEMON, CREAM AND DILL SAUCE

**2 medium (1kg) kohlrabi, halved, sliced**
**1 tablespoon olive oil**
**2 cloves garlic, crushed**
**300ml cream**
**2 tablespoons lemon juice**
**1 tablespoon chopped fresh dill**

Boil, steam or microwave kohlrabi until just tender; drain.

Heat oil in large pan; cook garlic, stirring, until fragrant. Stir in cream and lemon juice; simmer, uncovered, about 3 minutes or until sauce thickens slightly. Add kohlrabi and dill; simmer, uncovered, about 3 minutes or until kohlrabi is tender and sauce thickened, stirring occasionally during cooking.

Serves 4 to 6.

■ Best made just before serving.
■ Freeze: Not suitable.

## KOHLRABI WEDGES WITH SALSA FRESCA

**4 medium (2kg) kohlrabi**
**vegetable oil, for deep-frying**
**1½ teaspoons sweet paprika**
**½ teaspoon cayenne pepper**
**1 teaspoon salt**
**300ml sour cream**

SALSA FRESCA
**2 medium (380g) tomatoes, seeded, chopped**
**1 small (80g) onion, finely chopped**
**2 teaspoons chopped fresh parsley**
**1 teaspoon chopped fresh mint**
**1 tablespoon lemon juice**
**1 tablespoon olive oil**

Cut kohlrabi into 3cm wedges. Boil, steam or microwave until just tender; drain. Deep-fry kohlrabi in hot oil, in batches, until browned; drain on absorbent paper. Sprinkle kohlrabi with combined spices and salt; serve immediately, accompanied by sour cream and Salsa Fresca.

**Salsa Fresca:** Gently mix all ingredients in small bowl.

Serves 4 to 6.

■ Wedges best made just before serving. Salsa Fresca can be made a day ahead.
■ Storage: Covered, in refrigerator.
■ Freeze: Not suitable.

## HONEY-GLAZED KOHLRABI AND CARROTS

**3 medium (1.5kg) kohlrabi**
**2 large (360g) carrots**
**2 tablespoons water**
**2 tablespoons sugar**
**20g butter**
**1 tablespoon chopped fresh parsley**

Cut kohlrabi into 1.5cm slices; cut each slice into 2cm sticks. Quarter carrots lengthways; cut each quarter into 6cm lengths. Boil, steam or microwave kohlrabi and carrots, separately, until just tender; drain.

Heat water in large pan; add sugar, stir, without boiling, until sugar dissolves. Simmer about 1 minute or until syrup thickens slightly; add butter, stir until melted. Add kohlrabi and carrots; cook, stirring occasionally, until well glazed and browned lightly. Just before serving, stir in parsley.

Serves 6 to 8.

■ Best made just before serving.
■ Freeze: Not suitable.

# Kumara

*Known by its Polynesian name, this orange-fleshed sweet potato is neither potato nor yam but a tuberous relative of the morning glory vine. The nutty, rich taste of kumara is culinary proof that beauty is more than skin deep.*

Kumara

**COOKING METHODS** *Cooking times are based on 2 large (1kg) kumara, peeled, sliced into 2cm rounds.*

**BOIL** *Add kumara to large pan of boiling water; cook, uncovered, about 15 minutes or until tender. Drain.*

**STEAM** *Place kumara in steamer basket; cook, covered, over pan of simmering water about 16 minutes or until tender. Drain.*

**MICROWAVE** *Place kumara and 2 tablespoons water in large microwave-safe dish. Cover, microwave on HIGH (100%) about 10 minutes or until tender, pausing halfway during cooking time to stir. Drain.*

Tested in an 850-watt oven

## KUMARA AND BROCCOLI STIR-FRY

**3 medium (1.2kg) kumara, sliced**
**160g broccoli florets**
**1 tablespoon peanut oil**
**2 large (400g) onions, sliced**
**2 cloves garlic, crushed**
**2 teaspoons sambal oelek**

CUMIN YOGURT DRESSING
**½ cup (125ml) yogurt**
**½ teaspoon ground coriander**
**1 teaspoon ground cumin**
**1 tablespoon water**
**2 tablespoons lemon juice**

Boil, steam or microwave kumara and broccoli florets, separately, until almost tender; drain.

Meanwhile, heat oil in wok or large pan; stir-fry onions, garlic and sambal oelek until onions are browned lightly.

Add kumara and broccoli; stir-fry until vegetables are heated through. Just before serving, drizzle with Cumin Yogurt Dressing.

**Cumin Yogurt Dressing:** Combine all ingredients in small bowl.

Serves 6 to 8.

■ Cumin Yogurt Dressing can be made a day ahead.
■ Storage: Covered, in refrigerator.
■ Freeze: Not suitable.

*ABOVE: Kumara and Broccoli Stir-Fry.*
*OPPOSITE FROM TOP: Honey Mustard-Glazed Kumara; Cheese and Vegie Burgers.*

## HONEY MUSTARD-GLAZED KUMARA

2 large (1kg) kumara
2 medium (300g) onions, halved
½ cup (125ml) honey
2 tablespoons balsamic vinegar
2 tablespoons seeded mustard
1 tablespoon water
1 tablespoon peanut oil
1 tablespoon grated fresh ginger

Slice kumara into 1cm rounds. Place kumara and onions in large bowl; toss with combined honey, vinegar, mustard, water, oil and ginger. Drain vegetables; reserve honey-mustard mixture.

Place vegetables on wire rack over foil-covered oven tray; bake in moderately hot oven 20 minutes, brushing frequently with honey-mustard mixture. Turn vegetables; bake, about 15 minutes or until vegetables are browned lightly, continuing to brush with honey-mustard mixture during cooking.

Serves 4 to 6.

■ Best made just before serving.
■ Freeze: Not suitable.
■ Microwave: Not suitable.

## CHEESE AND VEGIE BURGERS

1 medium (400g) kumara, chopped
1 large (300g) potato, chopped
1 large (200g) onion, chopped
¼ cup (60ml) vegetable oil
⅓ cup (40g) grated cheddar cheese
80g green beans, chopped
¼ cup (15g) stale breadcrumbs
½ cup (85g) polenta

Combine kumara, potato, onion and 1 tablespoon of the oil in shallow baking dish; bake, covered, in moderate oven 30 minutes. Uncover, bake for a further 20 minutes or until vegetables are just tender. Transfer mixture to large bowl; mash until smooth. Stir in cheese, beans and breadcrumbs.

Sprinkle oven tray with half the polenta. Divide vegetable mash into 8 portions; press oiled metal 7.5cm egg ring into 1 portion, lift onto oven tray using spatula. Sprinkle polenta over burger; carefully remove egg ring. Repeat with remaining portions of vegetable mash.

Heat remaining oil in large pan; cook burgers, in batches, until browned both sides. Drain on absorbent paper.

Makes 8.

■ Burgers best made just before serving. Vegetable mash can be made a day ahead.
■ Storage: Covered, in refrigerator.
■ Freeze: Not suitable.
■ Microwave: Not suitable.

*Bowl from Villeroy & Boch*

*Plates from Villeroy & Boch*

# Salad Tips

- Keep lettuces under refrigeration until shortly before required. Wash lettuces carefully, spin or pat dry then place in a plastic bag, seal tightly and chill at least half an hour to crisp.

- Hand-held mixing wands are good for mixing dressings in a small jug or bowl rather than dirtying a blender or food processor.

## THOUSAND ISLAND DRESSING

*Prepared mayonnaise can be substituted for our homemade Basic Mayonnaise (see page 67).*

**1 cup (250ml) Basic Mayonnaise**
**1/4 cup (60ml) tomato sauce**
**1 tablespoon Worcestershire sauce**
**1/2 teaspoon Tabasco sauce**

Place ingredients in small bowl; whisk only until just combined.

Makes about 1 1/2 cups (375ml).

- Can be made a day ahead.
- Storage: Covered, in refrigerator.
- Freeze: Not suitable.

## BLUE CHEESE DRESSING

*Prepared mayonnaise can be substituted for our homemade Basic Mayonnaise (see page 67).*

**1 cup (250ml) Basic Mayonnaise**
**3/4 cup (180ml) cream**
**2 tablespoons white wine vinegar**
**200g firm blue-vein cheese, crumbled**

Blend or process all ingredients until just smooth.

Makes about 2 1/2 cups (625ml).

- Can be made a day ahead.
- Storage: Covered, in refrigerator.
- Freeze: Not suitable.

*Watercress:
Small, dark
leaves with
a sharp,
almost
bitter,
flavour.*

*Curly
Endive: A
cousin of
Chicory, with
a loose head of
fine, spidery,
slightly bitter,
pale leaves.*

*Iceberg:
Firm, large, round
head with crisp, pale-green
leaves having a clean, grassy taste.*

*Lamb's
Lettuce:
Also known as
Lamb's Tongue, Corn
Salad or Mâche, it has clusters of
tiny, tender, nutty-tasting leaves.*

# Lettuces

*What so many of us think of as lettuce is just the tip of
the iceberg – never before have we been so spoiled for
choice at the salad bar. With a mix of more than a dozen
different varieties of greens readily available, all
deservedly worth a fling, it's time to turn over a new leaf.*

## ITALIAN DRESSING

¼ cup (60ml) lemon juice
2 tablespoons white wine vinegar
1 teaspoon sugar
1 clove garlic, crushed
¾ cup (180ml) olive oil
1 teaspoon chopped fresh oregano
1 teaspoon chopped fresh thyme
1 teaspoon chopped fresh
    basil leaves
1 small fresh red chilli,
    coarsely chopped

Blend or process all ingredients until
just smooth.

Makes about 1¼ cups (310ml).

■ Can be made a day ahead.
■ Storage: Covered, in refrigerator.
■ Freeze: Not suitable.

## LOW-CALORIE DRESSING

¾ cup (45g) sun-dried tomatoes
    without oil
¾ cup (180ml) hot water
2 green onions, chopped
¾ cup (180ml) buttermilk
2 tablespoons roughly chopped
    fresh flat-leaf parsley
1 clove garlic, crushed
1 tablespoon lemon juice
1 teaspoon cracked black pepper

Combine tomatoes and water in bowl;
stand 10 minutes. Blend or process
undrained tomatoes with remaining
ingredients until just smooth.

Makes about 2 cups (500ml).

■ Can be made a day ahead.
■ Storage: Covered, in refrigerator.
■ Freeze: Not suitable.

## HONEY MUSTARD DRESSING

¾ cup (180ml) olive oil
2 tablespoons lemon juice
1 tablespoon seeded mustard
1 tablespoon honey

Blend or process all ingredients until
just smooth.

Makes about 1 cup (250ml).

■ Can be made a day ahead.
■ Storage: Covered, in refrigerator.
■ Freeze: Not suitable.

*CLOCKWISE FROM CENTRE TOP:
Italian Dressing; Thousand Island Dressing;
Blue Cheese Dressing; Honey Mustard
Dressing; Low-Calorie Dressing.*

# Lettuces

*Red Oak Leaf: With Green Oak also known as Leaf Lettuce because their delicate leaves can be picked off the plant one at a time.*

*Green Oak Leaf: Like the Red Oak, loosely packed, large-hearted lettuce with soft, gently frilled leaves and mild flavour.*

*Mesclun: Often sold as Mixed Small Leaves and consisting of an assortment of various edible greens and flowers.*

*Butter: Also known as Bibb or Boston Lettuce; large, mild-tasting, leaves so sweet and tender they're said to possess the luscious qualities of butter.*

*Red and Green Coral: Tightly furled, crunchy leaves with a mild, but distinct, taste.*

*CLOCKWISE FROM TOP: Caesar Dressing; French Dressing; Basic Mayonnaise; Pesto Dressing; Russian Salad Dressing.*

66

## PESTO DRESSING

**1/2 cup firmly packed
    fresh basil leaves**
**1/4 cup (20g) coarsely grated
    parmesan cheese**
**2 cloves garlic, crushed**
**2 tablespoons pine nuts, toasted**
**1 teaspoon cracked black pepper**
**3/4 cup (180ml) olive oil**
**1/4 cup (60ml) balsamic vinegar**

Blend or process all ingredients until just smooth.

Makes about 1 1/2 cups (375ml).

■ Can be made a day ahead.
■ Storage: Covered, in refrigerator.
■ Freeze: Not suitable.

## RUSSIAN SALAD DRESSING

*Prepared mayonnaise can be
substituted for our homemade Basic
Mayonnaise (see above right).*

**1 cup (250ml) Basic Mayonnaise**
**1/3 cup (80ml) mild chilli sauce**
**2 tablespoons chopped fresh chives**
**1/4 cup (40g) finely chopped
    pickled gherkin**

Blend or process all ingredients until just smooth.

Makes about 1 1/2 cups (375ml).

■ Can be made a day ahead.
■ Storage: Covered, in refrigerator.
■ Freeze: Not suitable.

## FRENCH DRESSING

**1/3 cup (80ml) olive oil**
**1/3 cup (80ml) vegetable oil**
**1/4 cup (60ml) white vinegar**
**1 teaspoon sugar**
**1 tablespoon Dijon mustard**
**1 clove garlic, crushed**

Blend or process all ingredients until just smooth.

Makes about 1 cup (250ml).

■ Can be made a day ahead.
■ Storage: Covered, in refrigerator.
■ Freeze: Not suitable.

## BASIC MAYONNAISE

**2 egg yolks**
**2 tablespoons lemon juice**
**2 teaspoons Dijon mustard**
**3/4 cup (180ml) extra light olive oil**

Blend or process yolks, juice and mustard until smooth. With motor operating, gradually pour in oil; process until thick.

Makes about 1 1/4 cups (310ml).

■ Can be made a day ahead.
■ Storage: Covered, in refrigerator.
■ Freeze: Not suitable.

## CAESAR DRESSING

*The way we have cooked the egg here
is the process meant when you see a
recipe calling for a coddled egg.*

**1 egg**
**8 anchovy fillets**
**2 cloves garlic, crushed**
**2 tablespoons lemon juice**
**1/2 cup (40g) grated
    parmesan cheese**
**1/2 teaspoon cracked black pepper**
**1/2 cup (125ml) olive oil**
**1/3 cup (80ml) cream**

Bring a small pan of water to boil. Add egg, immediately remove pan from heat; cover, allow to stand 3 minutes. Drain; cool egg under running water, peel over small bowl.

Blend or process egg with remaining ingredients until just smooth and thickened slightly.

Makes about 1 1/2 cups (375ml).

■ Can be made 3 hours ahead.
■ Storage: Covered, in refrigerator.
■ Freeze: Not suitable.

*Mizuna: Feathery green
leaves, edible pale
stems; distinctive
sharp flavour; from
Japan originally,
often used in
Mesclun mixes.*

*Mignonette: Deep
red or bright-green
tinged with red;
firm, crisp leaves
with a slightly bitter
taste. A good, all-
purpose salad
lettuce.*

*Cos and Baby Cos: Also called Romaine, this crisp,
elongated lettuce is the classic Caesar Salad green.*

# Mushrooms

*Sometimes called meat for vegetarians, mushrooms are high in protein, an excellent source of fibre, low in fat and high in vitamin content – one of nature's perfect products. And yummy into the bargain! Treat mushrooms gently, stored in a brown paper bag in the lowest part of your refrigerator, until ready to use them.*

*Swiss Brown:*
*A mild-tasting variety but more fully flavoured than Button, it is good in pasta dishes or cooked whole as it holds its shape. Light to dark brown with an earthy appearance, it is also known as Roman or Cremini.*

*Enoki:*
*Slender, 10cm-long body with a tiny head, it is creamy-yellow in colour and crisp in texture. Sold in clumps, it has a mild flavour and is good in stir-fries.*

## WARM MUSHROOM SALAD

100g butter
1/4 cup (60ml) olive oil
1 clove garlic, crushed
200g oyster mushrooms
200g Swiss brown mushrooms
100g shiitake mushrooms
125g mesclun [see Lettuce]
1 tablespoon lemon juice
1 tablespoon chopped fresh parsley

Heat half the butter and 1 tablespoon of the oil in large pan; cook garlic and mushrooms, stirring, until mushrooms are just tender. Line serving platter with mesclun; place mushroom mixture over leaves. Melt remaining butter; combine with remaining oil, lemon juice and parsley, drizzle over mushrooms.

Serves 4.

■ Best made just before serving.
■ Freeze: Not suitable.
■ Microwave: Suitable.

## ENOKI AND BUTTON MUSHROOM SALAD

2 tablespoons olive oil
1 clove garlic, crushed
250g button mushrooms, halved
100g enoki mushrooms
1/4 cup (35g) macadamia nuts, toasted, chopped
120g rocket
1 cup (80g) mung bean sprouts
1/4 cup (60ml) macadamia oil
2 tablespoons sweet chilli sauce
1 tablespoon chopped fresh coriander leaves
2 teaspoons lime juice

Heat oil in medium pan; cook garlic, stirring, 1 minute. Add button mushrooms; cook, stirring, until browned and just tender. Add enoki mushrooms; cook, stirring, until just wilted.

Gently toss mushrooms with nuts, rocket, sprouts and combined remaining ingredients in large bowl.

Serves 4.

■ Best made just before serving.
■ Freeze: Not suitable.
■ Microwave: Not suitable.

*Shiitake: One of the most cultivated mushrooms in the world, it is grey in colour and has a rich spicy flavour. Good eaten raw in salads.*

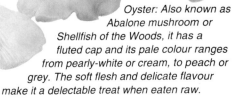

*Oyster: Also known as Abalone mushroom or Shellfish of the Woods, it has a fluted cap and its pale colour ranges from pearly-white or cream, to peach or grey. The soft flesh and delicate flavour make it a delectable treat when eaten raw.*

*OPPOSITE FROM TOP:*
*Enoki and Button Mushroom Salad;*

68

# Mushrooms

Bowl from Corso De' Fiori; plate from House In Newtown

## Cultivated Mushrooms

*Button: Smallest of the commercially cultivated common variety. Caps are closed; white in colour and mild in flavour, good in salads.*

*Cup: Subtle in flavour and firm, larger than Buttons with caps still closed. Good barbecued.*

*Flat: When fully open, they have a stronger flavour and are sometimes misnamed Field Mushrooms. They are good filled and barbecued, or as a complement to meat.*

## PROSCIUTTO-WRAPPED MUSHROOMS

*Hand-pick 16 fairly large, perfectly shaped mushrooms for this recipe.*

**1/2 cup (75g) sun-dried tomatoes in oil, drained**
**1/4 cup (20g) coarsely grated parmesan cheese**
**1 clove garlic, coarsely chopped**
**16 button mushrooms**
**8 slices (135g) prosciutto**

Blend or process tomatoes, parmesan and garlic until pureed. Carefully remove and discard stems from mushrooms; gently fill mushrooms with tomato mixture. Halve prosciutto slices lengthways; wrap 1 prosciutto strip around each mushroom. Cook under heated grill, turning once, until prosciutto is crisp and mushrooms are browned all over.

Serves 4.

■ Best cooked just before serving. Can be prepared a day ahead.
■ Storage: Covered, in refrigerator.
■ Freeze: Not suitable.

## MUSHROOMS A LA GRECQUE

**30g butter**
**1/3 cup (80ml) olive oil**
**1 clove garlic, crushed**
**500g button mushrooms, halved**
**1 tablespoon white wine vinegar**
**1 tablespoon chopped fresh oregano leaves**
**1 teaspoon Dijon mustard**

Heat butter and 1 tablespoon of the oil in medium pan; cook garlic, stirring, 1 minute. Add mushrooms; cook, stirring, until browned lightly and just tender. Transfer mixture to large bowl.

Combine remaining oil, vinegar, oregano and mustard in small bowl; pour over mushrooms. Cover; refrigerate at least 4 hours or overnight.

Serves 4.

■ Best made a day ahead.
■ Storage: Covered, in refrigerator.
■ Freeze: Not suitable.

## MUSHROOM, PEA AND POTATO KOFTA

2 teaspoons peanut oil
400g Swiss brown mushrooms, thinly sliced
2 green onions, sliced
1 tablespoon chopped fresh coriander leaves
1 teaspoon ground cumin
1 teaspoon ground coriander
1/2 teaspoon ground turmeric
1 teaspoon grated fresh ginger
1 large (300g) potato, finely grated, drained
1/4 cup (30g) frozen peas, cooked, drained
2 eggs, lightly beaten
1/4 cup (35g) plain flour
vegetable oil, for shallow-frying

Heat peanut oil in large pan; cook mushrooms, stirring, until browned and just tender. Cool. Combine mushrooms with onions, coriander, ground spices, ginger, potato, peas, eggs and flour in large bowl. Heat enough vegetable oil to come to 1cm-depth in medium pan. Place 4 egg rings in pan, spoon 1/4 cup (60ml) of mixture into rings; cook until browned on both sides. Drain on absorbent paper; repeat with remaining mixture. Serve with yogurt, if desired.

Serves 4 to 6.

■ Best made just before serving.
■ Freeze: Not suitable.
■ Microwave: Not suitable.

## MALABAR MUSHROOM CURRY

1 tablespoon peanut oil
2 cloves garlic, crushed
2 teaspoons grated fresh ginger
2 teaspoons brown mustard seeds
2 teaspoons coriander seeds
2 teaspoons cumin seeds
1/2 teaspoon ground turmeric
1 cup (250ml) coconut cream
650g flat mushrooms, finely sliced
1 tablespoon chopped fresh coriander leaves

Heat oil in wok or large pan; stir-fry garlic, ginger, seeds and turmeric about 1 minute or until fragrant. Add half the coconut cream; boil, stirring, until mixture starts to thicken. Add mushrooms and remaining coconut cream; cook, stirring, for about 4 minutes or until mushrooms are just tender. Just before serving, sprinkle with coriander leaves.

Serves 4.

■ Best made just before serving.
■ Freeze: Not suitable.
■ Microwave: Not suitable.

*OPPOSITE FROM TOP: Mushrooms à la Grecque; Prosciutto-Wrapped Mushrooms. BELOW FROM TOP: Malabar Mushroom Curry; Mushroom, Pea and Potato Kofta.*

# Mushrooms

*Plate from Albi Imports*

## MUSHROOM RISOTTO

**1.5 litres (6 cups) chicken stock**
**½ cup (125ml) dry white wine**
**2 tablespoons olive oil**
**30g butter**
**500g button mushrooms, sliced**
**2 cloves garlic, crushed**
**2 cups (400g) arborio rice**
**    [see Glossary]**
**½ cup (125ml) cream**
**½ cup (40g) coarsely grated**
**    parmesan cheese**

Bring stock and wine, uncovered, to boil in large pan; cover, reduce heat to low.

Heat oil and butter in large pan; cook mushrooms and garlic, stirring, until mushrooms are tender. Add rice; stir for 1 minute. Add ²/₃ cup (160ml) hot stock mixture to rice mixture; cook, stirring, until liquid is absorbed. Continue adding stock mixture, in batches, stirring until absorbed between each addition. Cooking time, from when the first liquid is added, should be about 35 minutes, or until rice is tender and creamy. Stir in cream; cook, stirring, until cream is absorbed and risotto starts to thicken. Stir in parmesan; serve immediately.

Serves 4.

■ Best made just before serving.
■ Freeze: Not suitable.
■ Microwave: Suitable.

## MUSHROOM AND LEEK FRITTATA

**1 tablespoon olive oil**
**20g butter**
**2 cloves garlic, crushed**
**1 small (200g) leek, thinly sliced**
**250g Swiss brown**
**    mushrooms, sliced**
**200g button mushrooms, sliced**
**6 eggs**
**½ cup (125ml) cream**
**½ cup (40g) finely grated**
**    parmesan cheese**
**1 tablespoon chopped fresh parsley**

Oil and line base 23cm slab pan with baking paper.

Heat oil and butter in large pan; cook garlic, leek and mushrooms, stirring, until mushrooms are tender. Cool; spread mushroom mixture over base of prepared pan. Whisk eggs, cream, parmesan and parsley in large jug; pour over mushroom mixture in pan. Bake, uncovered, in moderate oven about 45 minutes or until set. Cool in pan; cut into triangles.

Serves 6 to 8.

■ Can be made a day ahead.
■ Storage: Covered, in refrigerator.
■ Freeze: Not suitable.
■ Microwave: Not suitable.

*ABOVE FROM TOP: Mushroom and Leek Frittata; Mushroom Risotto.*
*OPPOSITE: Stir-Fried Mixed Mushrooms.*

# STIR-FRIED MIXED MUSHROOMS

8 Chinese dried mushrooms
1 tablespoon peanut oil
2 cloves garlic, crushed
2 teaspoons finely grated
 fresh ginger
100g black fungi
150g shimeji mushrooms
425g can straw mushrooms, drained
200g broccoli florets
500g choy sum, chopped
2 baby bok choy, chopped
¼ cup (60ml) light soy sauce
2 tablespoons sweet chilli sauce
1 tablespoon oyster sauce
1 tablespoon rice vinegar

Cover dried mushrooms in small bowl with boiling water; stand 20 minutes. Drain; remove and discard mushroom stems, slice caps thinly.

Heat oil in wok or large pan; stir-fry garlic, ginger and all mushrooms for 1 minute. Add broccoli, choy sum and bok choy; stir-fry 2 minutes. Add combined sauces and vinegar; stir-fry until choy sum and bok choy are just wilted and sauce comes to boil.

Serves 4 to 6.

■ Best made just
 before serving.
■ Freeze: Not suitable.
■ Microwave: Not suitable.

*Black Fungus: Also known as Cloud Ear; originally a tree fungus but now cultivated on wood in steam rooms; should be just briefly cooked.*

*Shimeji: Resemble Oyster mushrooms but are grown in clusters on banks of cottonseed hull. Colour fades as they mature, ranging from off-white to woody brown; firm texture, mild flavour and succulent.*

# Mushrooms

## MUSHROOM-FILLED BABY BOK CHOY

**6 Chinese dried mushrooms**
**6 baby bok choy**
**2 tablespoons peanut oil**
**500g button mushrooms,**
   **finely chopped**
**2 cloves garlic, crushed**
**2 teaspoons grated fresh ginger**
**2 tablespoons light soy sauce**
**1 tablespoon oyster sauce**
**1 teaspoon sesame oil**

Cover dried mushrooms in small bowl with boiling water; stand 20 minutes. Drain; discard mushroom stems, chop caps finely. Carefully cut each bok choy lengthways, no more than about three-quarters of the way through; open each bok choy gently, so it forms a V-shape.

Heat 1 tablespoon of the oil in wok or large pan; stir-fry both mushrooms, garlic and ginger until mushrooms are soft and almost all liquid is evaporated. Add combined sauces; stir-fry until mixture comes to the boil. Remove from heat; cool mixture 5 minutes.

Divide filling mixture among bok choy; tie kitchen string [see Glossary] around each bok choy, about 7cm from ends of leaves, to enclose filling. Place bok choy, in single layer, in large bamboo steamer over wok or large pan of simmering water; steam, covered, about 5 minutes or until bok choy are tender and filling is heated through. Drizzle with combined heated remaining peanut oil and sesame oil before serving.

Serves 6.

■ Best made just before serving.
■ Freeze: Not suitable.
■ Microwave: Suitable.

## BARBECUED MUSHROOMS WITH HERB BUTTER

**100g butter, melted**
**1 teaspoon grated lime rind**
**1 tablespoon lime juice**
**1 tablespoon chopped fresh parsley**
**1 tablespoon chopped fresh**
   **basil leaves**
**6 large flat mushrooms**

Combine butter, rind, juice, parsley and basil in small bowl. Cook mushrooms in heated oiled griddle pan (or grill or barbecue), brushing with half of the butter mixture, until mushrooms are just tender and well browned. Serve accompanied with remaining butter mixture.

Serves 6.

■ Butter mixture can be made
   a day ahead.
■ Storage: Covered, in refrigerator.
■ Freeze: Not suitable.
■ Microwave: Butter mixture suitable.

## ROASTED MUSHROOMS

**500g button mushrooms**
**500g Swiss brown mushrooms**
**3 cloves garlic, crushed**
**½ cup (125ml) olive oil**
**2 teaspoons salt**
**½ teaspoon freshly ground**
   **black pepper**

Combine all ingredients in large bowl; place mixture in single layer in baking dish. Bake, uncovered, in hot oven about 20 minutes or until mushrooms are very soft and browned lightly.

Serves 4 to 6.

■ Best made just before serving.
■ Freeze: Not suitable.
■ Microwave: Not suitable.

## MUSHROOM AND ZUCCHINI LASAGNE

2 medium (240g) zucchini
1 tablespoon olive oil
1 medium (150g) onion, chopped
2 cloves garlic, crushed
500g button mushrooms, sliced
2 cups (500ml) tomato-based
    pasta sauce
4 (100g) instant lasagne sheets
2½ cups (500g) ricotta cheese
½ cup (40g) coarsely grated
    parmesan cheese

Using a vegetable peeler, cut zucchini into thin strips; place on wire rack over tray, sprinkle with salt, stand 20 minutes. Rinse zucchini under cold water; pat dry with absorbent paper. Cook zucchini in heated oiled griddle pan until tender and browned on both sides.

Heat oil in large pan; cook onion, garlic and mushrooms, stirring, until mushrooms are soft. Cool; drain, discarding juices from mushrooms.

Spread base of 2-litre (8-cup) oven-proof dish with a quarter of the pasta sauce; top with 2 sheets of the lasagne, mushroom mixture, ricotta, half of the remaining sauce, then zucchini. Cover with remaining lasagne sheets; spread remaining sauce over lasagne, sprinkle with parmesan. Bake, uncovered, in moderate oven about 45 minutes or until pasta is tender; cover with foil if surface starts to overbrown. Stand 5 minutes before serving.

Serves 8.

▨ Best made on day of serving.
▨ Storage: Covered, in refrigerator.
▨ Freeze: Not suitable.
▨ Microwave: Not suitable.

*Polka-dot plate from The Bay Tree Kitchen Shop*

## MUSHROOM RATATOUILLE

1 tablespoon olive oil
1 large (200g) onion, sliced
2 cloves garlic, crushed
600g button mushrooms
2 medium (240g) zucchini, sliced
2 (120g) baby eggplants, sliced
1 small (150g) green capsicum,
    seeded, chopped
400g can tomatoes,
    undrained, crushed
¼ cup (60ml) tomato paste
½ cup (125ml) chicken stock
¼ cup (60ml) dry red wine
1 tablespoon balsamic vinegar
1 tablespoon chopped
    fresh oregano

Heat oil in large pan; cook onion and garlic, stirring, until onion is soft. Add mushrooms, zucchini, eggplants and capsicum; cook, stirring until vegetables are just tender.

Add tomatoes, paste, stock and wine; simmer, uncovered, about 15 minutes or until mixture thickens and vegetables are soft. Just before serving, stir in vinegar and oregano.

Serves 4 to 6.

▨ Can be made a day ahead.
▨ Storage: Covered, in refrigerator.
▨ Freeze: Not suitable.
▨ Microwave: Not suitable.

*OPPOSITE FROM TOP: Roasted Mushrooms; Barbecued Mushrooms with Herb Butter.*
*LEFT: Mushroom-Filled Baby Bok Choy.*
*ABOVE FROM TOP: Mushroom Ratatouille; Mushroom and Zucchini Lasagne.*

## Okra Tips

- To avoid its viscous properties, leave the okra whole when cooking them and take care not to slice off the stem too close to the flesh when trimming.

- Use the smallest, greenest okra available, and scrub away as much of the fuzz on the skin as possible.

## OKRA WITH TOMATOES

2 tablespoons olive oil
2 medium (300g) onions,
  thinly sliced
2 cloves garlic, crushed
2 x 400g cans tomatoes,
  undrained, crushed
500g okra
1 teaspoon sugar
¼ cup (60ml) tomato paste
¼ cup (60ml) dry red wine
1 tablespoon chopped
  fresh oregano

Heat oil in large pan; cook onions and garlic, stirring, until onions are soft. Add all remaining ingredients; simmer, uncovered, about 30 minutes or until okra is tender.

Serves 4 to 6.

- Can be made a day ahead.
- Storage: Covered, in refrigerator.
- Freeze: Not suitable.
- Microwave: Not suitable.

*CLOCKWISE FROM TOP: Okra with Tomatoes; Crunchy Cajun Okra with Chilli Mayonnaise; Masala Okra.*

# Okra

*Okra is one of those flavoursome yet misunderstood vegetables which when handled properly rewards the cook immensely. A native of Africa, okra was transported, along with the slaves, to the USA's Deep South where it became a staple ingredient in Creole cooking, particularly in many a delicious gumbo.*

*All bowls and tray from Home & Garden on the Mall*

Okra

### MASALA OKRA

2 tablespoons ghee
2 medium (300g) onions,
   thinly sliced
2 teaspoons grated fresh ginger
2 cloves garlic, crushed
1 teaspoon black mustard seeds
1 small fresh red chilli, thinly sliced
1 teaspoon garam masala
2 teaspoons ground cumin
500g okra
1 cup (250ml) water
½ cup (125ml) coconut milk
1 tablespoon chopped fresh
   coriander leaves

Heat ghee in large pan; cook onions, ginger and garlic, stirring, until onions are soft. Add seeds, chilli and spices; cook, stirring, until fragrant. Add okra and water; simmer, uncovered, about 30 minutes or until okra is soft and liquid evaporated. Add coconut milk and coriander; stir until heated through.

Serves 4 to 6.

■ Can be made a day ahead.
■ Storage: Covered, in refrigerator.
■ Freeze: Not suitable.
■ Microwave: Not suitable.

### CRUNCHY CAJUN OKRA WITH CHILLI MAYONNAISE

500g okra
plain flour
3 eggs, lightly beaten
1 cup (170g) polenta
2 tablespoons Cajun seasoning
2 teaspoons chicken salt
   [see Glossary]
vegetable oil, for deep-frying

CHILLI MAYONNAISE
1 egg
1 tablespoon lime juice
1 clove garlic, crushed
1 cup (250ml) light olive oil
1 tablespoon chopped fresh
   coriander leaves
1 tablespoon sambal oelek

Coat okra with flour, shake away excess; dip into eggs, then coat with combined polenta, seasoning and salt. Deep-fry okra in hot oil, in batches, until golden brown and tender (watch that oil is not so hot that okra overbrowns before it is cooked through). Serve with Chilli Mayonnaise.

**Chilli Mayonnaise:** Blend or process egg, juice and garlic until smooth. With motor operating, gradually pour in oil; process until thick. Stir in coriander and sambal oelek.

Serves 4 to 6.

■ Chilli Mayonnaise can be made
   a day ahead.
■ Storage: Covered, in refrigerator.
■ Freeze: Not suitable.
■ Microwave: Not suitable.

# Onions

*Members of the onion family are usually regarded as the workhorses of the kitchen, basic rather than main ingredients... what a waste of fabulous flavours, amazing versatility and endless possibilities. Knowing your onions means using them, cooked and raw, as heroes in your culinary adventures so that you can create a mouthwatering collection of truly epic proportions.*

Chives

Garlic

Red Onion

Brown Onion

White Onion

Green Onion

Spring Onion

Shallots

Pickling Onions

Leek

Garlic Chives

## DYNAMITE FRIED ONION RINGS

4 medium (600g) brown onions
½ cup (75g) plain flour
½ cup (75g) cornflour
2 tablespoons Cajun seasoning
  [see Glossary]
¾ cup (180ml) water
1 egg
vegetable oil, for deep-frying
1 cup (250ml) sour cream
¼ cup (60ml) hot chilli sauce
2 tablespoons chopped fresh
  coriander leaves
1 tablespoon lime juice
1 clove garlic, crushed
2 teaspoons grated lime rind

Cut onions into 1cm slices; separate into rings. Add onion rings to medium pan of boiling water; when water re-boils, drain immediately. Pat onion rings dry with absorbent paper.

Combine flours and seasoning in medium bowl; whisk in combined water and egg until smooth. Dip rings, a few at a time, into batter; deep-fry rings in hot oil, in batches, until crisp and browned lightly. Drain on absorbent paper. Serve onion rings with dipping sauce made of combined remaining ingredients.

Serves 4 to 6.

■ Onions must be made just before serving. Dipping sauce can be made a day ahead.
■ Storage: Sauce, covered, in refrigerator.
■ Freeze: Not suitable.
■ Microwave: Not suitable.

## MEXICAN-STYLE BARBECUED ONIONS

4 medium (680g) red onions
35g packet taco seasoning
1 large (320g) avocado
2 teaspoons lemon juice
½ small (40g) onion, finely chopped
few drops Tabasco sauce
⅓ cup (80ml) sour cream
1 tablespoon chopped fresh
  coriander leaves

Cut onions into 1.5cm slices; coat slices with seasoning. Cook slices, in batches, in a heated oiled griddle pan (or grill or barbecue) until browned both sides and tender. Meanwhile, place avocado in medium bowl, mash roughly with a fork; stir in lemon juice, onion and Tabasco.

Serve onions topped with avocado mixture, sour cream and coriander.

Serves 4 to 6.

■ Best made just before serving.
■ Freeze: Not suitable.
■ Microwave: Not suitable.

*OPPOSITE FROM LEFT:*
*Mexican-Style Barbecued Onions;*
*Dynamite Fried Onion Rings.*

## SWEET AND SOUR LEEKS

**3 large (1.5kg) leeks
2 tablespoons vegetable oil
40g butter
½ cup (125ml) lemon juice
2 tablespoons sugar**

Halve each leek lengthways; halve each piece crossways. Secure each piece with a toothpick.

Heat oil and butter in large shallow pan; cook leeks, over low heat, until tender and browned lightly, turning occasionally. Remove leeks from pan; keep warm. Add juice and sugar to same pan, bring to boil; simmer, stirring, about 5 minutes or until sauce reduces to a syrupy consistency. Pour sauce over leeks.

Serves 4.

■ Best made just before serving.
■ Freeze: Not suitable.
■ Microwave: Not suitable.

*Platter and cover from Corso De' Fiori*

*Green bowl from The Bay Tree Kitchen Shop*

*Polka dot plate from The Bay Tree Kitchen Shop*

## ONIONS AND TOMATOES PROVENÇALE

**12 small (960g) brown onions, halved**
**1 medium (70g) bulb garlic, unpeeled**
**4 large (360g) egg tomatoes, quartered**
**3 sprigs fresh rosemary**
**3 sprigs fresh thyme**
**1/3 cup (80ml) olive oil**
**1/4 cup (60ml) red wine vinegar**
**1 tablespoon brown sugar**

Combine onions, garlic, tomatoes, herbs and half the oil in large bowl; spread mixture in flameproof baking dish. Bake, uncovered, in moderately slow oven about 2 hours or until vegetables are tender, turning twice during cooking time. Remove onions and tomatoes to serving dish.

Squeeze pulp from 5 of the garlic cloves into same baking dish; discard remaining garlic and herbs. Add remaining oil, vinegar and sugar to same dish; cook, stirring, about 10 minutes or until sauce reduces slightly. Pour sauce over onions and tomatoes.

Serves 4 to 6.

■ Best made just before serving.
■ Freeze: Not suitable.
■ Microwave: Not suitable.

## WHITE BEAN AND GARLIC PUREE

**1 cup (200g) dried cannellini beans**
**4 large cloves garlic, coarsely chopped**
**2 tablespoons white vinegar**
**1 tablespoon lemon juice**
**1/3 cup (80ml) olive oil**

Cover beans in medium bowl with cold water; stand overnight.

Drain beans, transfer to medium pan of cold water. Bring to boil; simmer, covered, about 2 hours or until beans are tender. Drain. Blend or process beans, garlic, vinegar and juice until smooth. With motor operating, gradually pour in oil; process until pureed.

Serves 4 to 6.

■ Can be made a day ahead.
■ Storage: Covered, in refrigerator.
■ Freeze: Not suitable.
■ Microwave: Not suitable.

## CARAMELISED MIXED ONIONS

**1 large (90g) bulb garlic**
**50g butter**
**2 tablespoons olive oil**
**24 shallots**
**6 spring onions, halved**
**10 green onions, halved**
**1 tablespoon balsamic vinegar**

Separate garlic bulb into cloves; peel cloves. Heat butter and oil in large pan; cook garlic, shallots and spring onions about 45 minutes, stirring, until tender and browned. Add green onions; cook, stirring, until just tender. Drizzle with vinegar; serve immediately.

Serves 4 to 6.

■ Best made just before serving.
■ Freeze: Not suitable.
■ Microwave: Not suitable.

*OPPOSITE ABOVE: Sweet and Sour Leeks.*
*OPPOSITE FROM LEFT: Onions and Tomatoes Provençale; White Bean and Garlic Puree.*
*ABOVE: Caramelised Mixed Onions.*

# Parsnips

*This simple white root vegetable undergoes a change in flavour with the first sign of cold weather when its starch is converted to sugar, resulting in the distinctive sweet earthiness that marries so well with the Sunday roast.*

*Parsnip*

## COOKING METHODS
*Cooking times are based on 4 medium (500g) parsnips, peeled, roughly chopped.*

**BOIL** *Add parsnips to large pan of boiling water; boil, uncovered, about 8 minutes or until tender. Drain.*

**STEAM** *Place parsnips in steamer basket; cook, covered, over pan of simmering water about 8 minutes or until tender. Drain.*

**MICROWAVE** *Place parsnips and 2 tablespoons water in large microwave-safe dish. Cover, microwave on HIGH (100%) about 6 minutes or until tender, pausing halfway during cooking time to turn. Drain.*
Tested in an 850-watt oven

## OVEN-BAKED PARSNIP CHIPS
**6 medium (750g) parsnips**
**1 teaspoon salt**
**1/3 cup (80ml) olive oil**
**2 sprigs fresh rosemary**
**6 large cloves garlic, unpeeled**
**1/4 teaspoon sweet paprika**

Using a crinkle cutter or sharp knife, cut parsnips into thick slices; cut slices into 6cm-long chips.

Toss chips with combined remaining ingredients in large bowl; place coated chips in single layer in baking dish. Bake, uncovered, in moderately hot oven about 45 minutes or until chips are browned and crisp, turning occasionally.

Serves 4.
■ Best made just before serving.
■ Freeze: Not suitable.
■ Microwave: Not suitable.

## PARSNIP AND CARROT RIBBONS

**2 large (360g) parsnips**
**2 large (360g) carrots**
**vegetable oil, for deep-frying**

Using a vegetable peeler, peel thin strips from parsnips and carrots. Heat oil in large pan; deep-fry parsnip and carrot strips, separately, in batches, until browned and crisp. Drain on absorbent paper; serve immediately.

Serves 4.

■ Must be made just before serving.
■ Freeze: Not suitable.
■ Microwave: Not suitable.

## PARSNIP, KUMARA AND SPINACH PARFAIT

**6 medium (750g) parsnips, chopped**
**2 medium (800g) kumara, chopped**
**1 cup (250ml) hot buttermilk**
**40g butter, melted**
**½ cup (40g) coarsely grated parmesan cheese**
**1 small (80g) onion, chopped**
**3 bacon rashers, chopped**
**250g baby English spinach leaves, shredded**

Boil, steam or microwave parsnips and kumara, separately, until tender; drain. Blend or process parsnips until pureed; push puree through fine sieve into large bowl. Stir half the buttermilk, butter and cheese into puree; cover to keep warm.

Mash kumara; push mash through fine sieve into separate large bowl. Stir remaining buttermilk, butter and cheese into kumara mash; cover to keep warm.

Cook onion and bacon in large pan until bacon is crisp; stir in spinach, cook until just wilted.

Swirl parsnip puree, kumara mash and spinach mixture, in layers, in a serving dish.

Serves 4 to 6.

■ Best made just before serving.
■ Freeze: Not suitable.

*OPPOSITE FROM TOP: Parsnip, Kumara and Spinach Parfait; Oven-Baked Parsnip Chips.*
*ABOVE: Parsnip and Carrot Ribbons.*

# Green Peas

**COOKING METHODS** *Cooking times are based on 500g fresh green peas, shelled (approximately 1¼ cups).*

**BOIL** *Add green peas to small pan of boiling water; boil, uncovered, about 5 minutes or until tender. Drain.*

**STEAM** *Place green peas in steamer basket; cook, covered, over pan of simmering water about 3 minutes or until tender. Drain.*

**MICROWAVE** *Place green peas and 1 tablespoon water in large microwave-safe dish. Cover, microwave on HIGH (100%) about 3 minutes or until tender, pausing halfway during cooking time to stir. Drain.*
Tested in an 830-watt oven

## GREEN PEA MASH WITH KIPFLERS

*You need approximately 2.5kg of unshelled green peas (about 1kg shelled peas) for this recipe. Buy medium-sized, similar-shaped kipflers to make the finished dish appealing in appearance.*

**18 (900g) kipfler potatoes
    [see Potatoes]**
**6 cups shelled green peas**
**¼ cup (20g) finely grated
    parmesan cheese**
**⅓ cup (80ml) cream**
**1 teaspoon cracked black pepper**
**¼ cup (20g) parmesan
    cheese flakes**

Boil, steam or microwave potatoes and peas, separately, until just tender; drain.

Blend or process peas with grated parmesan, cream and pepper until pureed. Place 3 potatoes on individual serving plates; press each with potato masher to break skin, top with pea puree and flaked parmesan.

Serves 6.

■ Best made just before serving.
■ Freeze: Not suitable.

*RIGHT: Green Pea Mash with Kipflers.
OPPOSITE FROM TOP LEFT:
Quartet of Peas in Minted Coriander Butter;
Sugar Snap Peas with Toasted Pecans.*

Snow Pea
Sprouts

Green Peas

# Peas

The pea is believed to have been cultivated in prehistory, and its seeds were found in ancient Egyptian tombs. It has stood the test of time because it tastes of spring, and its tender pods, delicate tendrils and white flowers make it visually appealing. And besides, pea stands for perfect.

## Sugar Snap & Snow Peas

**COOKING METHODS** *Cooking times are based on 250g sugar snap peas or snow peas, ends trimmed, strings removed.*

**BOIL** *Add peas to small pan of boiling water; boil, uncovered, about 2 minutes or until tender. Drain.*

**STEAM** *Place peas in steamer basket; cook, covered, over pan of simmering water about 3 minutes or until tender. Drain.*

**MICROWAVE** *Place peas and 2 teaspoons water in large microwave-safe dish. Cover, microwave on HIGH (100%) about 2 minutes or until tender, pausing halfway during cooking time to stir. Drain.*

Tested in an 830-watt oven

### SUGAR SNAP PEAS WITH TOASTED PECANS

**60g butter**
**2 tablespoons lemon juice**
**1 tablespoon brown sugar**
**1 tablespoon cracked black pepper**
**1/4 cup (30g) chopped pecans, toasted**
**600g sugar snap peas**

Heat butter in medium pan; cook remaining ingredients about 3 minutes or until peas are just tender, stirring frequently.

Serves 4 to 6.

■ Best made just before serving.
■ Freeze: Not suitable.
■ Microwave: Suitable.

*Sugar Snap Peas*

*Snow Peas*

Place setting from House in Newtown

### QUARTET OF PEAS IN MINTED CORIANDER BUTTER

**1¼ cups (500g) shelled green peas**
**200g snow peas**
**200g sugar snap peas**
**60g snow pea sprouts**

MINTED CORIANDER BUTTER
**2 teaspoons vegetable oil**
**1 medium (150g) onion, chopped**
**1 clove garlic, crushed**

**1/3 cup coarsely chopped fresh mint leaves**
**1/3 cup coarsely chopped fresh coriander leaves**
**60g butter, softened**

Boil, steam or microwave shelled green peas, snow peas and sugar snap peas, separately, until just tender; drain. Combine peas with sprouts and Minted Coriander Butter; serve immediately.

**Minted Coriander Butter:** Heat oil in small pan; cook onion and garlic, stirring, until onion is soft. Cool. Blend or process onion mixture with remaining ingredients until pureed.

Serves 4 to 6.

■ Best made just before serving.
■ Freeze: Minted Coriander Butter suitable.

# Potatoes

**King Edward:** Slightly plump and rosy; great mashed.

**Tiny New Potatoes:** Also known as Chats. Not a variety but an early harvest with a thin, pale skin that's easily rubbed off. Good steamed, and eaten hot or cold in salads.

**Kipfler:** Small and finger-shaped; it has a nutty flavour, and is great baked and in salads.

**Desiree:** Oval-shaped with a smooth, pink skin and waxy, yellow flesh. Good both boiled and roasted, it's also one of the best for mashing.

**Pink Fir Apple:** Elongated with a rosy skin and waxy flesh; is good boiled, baked and in salads.

**Pontiac:** Large and round, it has a red skin marked with deep eyes, and the flesh is white. Good grated, boiled and baked.

**Congo:** Small and elongated with purple skin and flesh; sweet and floury, best used fried for chips.

**Idaho:** Also known as Russet Burbank; ruddy colour, fabulous baked and fried.

*One potato, two potato, three potato, four... but who would have dreamed that the "more" we counted up to would one day exceed the 30 varieties now grown in this country? Fried, mashed, roasted, boiled or baked, the potato is the most widely cooked of all vegetables, tastes great, is virtually fat-free and is a good source of fibre – no wonder its absence could start a revolution.*

## COOKING METHODS

*Cooking times are based on 5 medium (1kg) potatoes, peeled, quartered.*

**BOIL** *Add potatoes to large pan of boiling water; boil, uncovered, about 15 minutes or until tender. Drain.*

**STEAM** *Place potatoes in steamer basket; cook, covered, over pan of simmering water about 20 minutes or until tender. Drain.*

**MICROWAVE** *Place potatoes and 2 tablespoons water in large microwave-safe dish. Cover, microwave on HIGH (100%) about 10 minutes or until tender, pausing halfway during cooking time to stir. Drain.*

Tested in an 850-watt oven

## NICE 'N' SPICY WEDGES

5 large russet burbank potatoes
1 tablespoon cornflour
5 tablespoons ghee
1 medium (150g) onion, finely chopped
2 cloves garlic, crushed
2 teaspoons grated fresh ginger
1 teaspoon brown mustard seeds
1 teaspoon cumin seeds
2 teaspoons garam masala
1/2 teaspoon chilli powder
1 teaspoon sumac [see Glossary]
1 teaspoon salt
1/4 cup (60ml) lemon juice
2 tablespoons finely chopped fresh coriander leaves

Halve potatoes lengthways; cut each half into 3 wedges. Boil, steam or microwave potatoes until almost tender; drain. When cool, toss potatoes in cornflour.

Heat about 1 tablespoon of the ghee in medium pan; cook onion, garlic and ginger, stirring, until onion is soft. Add seeds, garam masala and chilli; cook, stirring, until fragrant. Remove from heat, stir in sumac and salt.

Heat half remaining ghee in large pan; cook half the potatoes about 5 minutes or until browned and crisp all sides. Remove from pan, keep warm; repeat with remaining ghee and potatoes.

Toss all potatoes together in same pan with reserved spice mixture, juice and coriander leaves.

Serves 6.

■ Best made just before serving.
■ Freeze: Not suitable.

*OPPOSITE: Nice 'N' Spicy Wedges.*

# Potatoes

## ROASTED POTATO SALAD WITH BASIL MAYONNAISE

**1kg tiny new potatoes, unpeeled**
**2 tablespoons olive oil**
**200g button mushrooms, sliced**
**1/3 cup (50g) sun-dried tomatoes in oil, drained, sliced**
**1/3 cup (50g) pine nuts, toasted**
**2 tablespoons shredded fresh basil leaves**

BASIL MAYONNAISE
**3 egg yolks**
**3 cloves garlic, coarsely chopped**
**1 tablespoon Dijon mustard**
**1/4 cup (60ml) white wine vinegar**
**3/4 cup (180ml) olive oil**
**1/3 cup firmly packed fresh basil leaves, shredded**
**1/4 teaspoon freshly ground black pepper**

Place potatoes in baking dish, drizzle with half the oil; bake, uncovered, in moderate oven, about 45 minutes or until potatoes are tender.

Meanwhile, heat remaining oil in large pan; cook mushrooms, stirring, about 4 minutes or until browned. Gently toss warm potatoes and mushrooms with tomatoes, pine nuts, basil and Basil Mayonnaise in large bowl.

**Basil Mayonnaise:** Blend or process egg yolks, garlic, mustard and vinegar until smooth. With motor operating, gradually pour in oil; process until thick. Add basil and pepper; process briefly. Makes about 2 cups (500ml).

Serves 4 to 6.

■ Roasted Potato Salad best made just before serving. Mayonnaise can be made a day ahead.
■ Storage: Covered, in refrigerator.
■ Freeze: Not suitable.
■ Microwave: Not suitable.

## POTATO FATTOUSH

*Fattoush, the Syrian and Lebanese deliciously healthy salad that cleverly uses yesterday's bread as a main ingredient, is even more substantial with the addition of potatoes.*

**1.5kg desiree potatoes, unpeeled**
**2 large pieces pitta bread**
**2 cups firmly packed fresh flat-leaf parsley, coarsely chopped**
**1 medium (150g) onion, thinly sliced**
**4 large (360g) egg tomatoes, chopped**
**2 medium (260g) Lebanese cucumbers, thinly sliced**
**1/4 cup fresh mint leaves, coarsely chopped**
**2/3 cup (160ml) light olive oil**
**1/2 cup (125ml) lemon juice**
**1/2 teaspoon freshly ground black pepper**

Pink-Eye: Small with off-white skin and deep purple eyes; good steamed, boiled and baked.

Spunta: Large, long, yellow-fleshed and floury; great mashed and fried.

Bintje: Oval-shaped with a creamy skin and yellow flesh; great baked and fried, good in salads.

Sebago: White skin, oval-shaped; good fried, mashed and baked.

*Bowls from Prima Cosa; tray from Lime Bay*

## TRI-FRIES WITH CHILLI SALT

**1 medium (400g) kumara, unpeeled**
**1 medium (400g) white sweet**
**potato, unpeeled**
**2 medium (400g) new**
**potatoes, unpeeled**
**vegetable oil, for deep-frying**
**1½ teaspoons salt**
**¼ teaspoon hot chilli powder**
**¼ teaspoon freshly cracked**
**black pepper**

Scrub all potatoes; pat dry. Using a V-slicer, slice potatoes very thinly. Heat oil in large pan; deep-fry slices, in batches, until golden brown and crisp, drain on absorbent paper. Sprinkle hot fries with combined remaining ingredients and serve immediately.

Serves 6.

■ Must be made just before serving.
■ Freeze: Not suitable.
■ Microwave: Not suitable.

Boil, steam or microwave potatoes until just tender; drain. When cool enough to handle, peel; cut into 2cm pieces.

Split each pitta in half; toast in hot oven until crisp. Break pitta halves into small, even-size pieces. Combine pitta pieces with potatoes, parsley, onion, tomatoes and cucumbers in large bowl. Just before serving, pour combined remaining ingredients over fattoush mixture; toss gently to combine.

Serves 6 to 8.

■ Best made just before serving.
■ Freeze: Not suitable.

*ABOVE FROM LEFT: Roasted Potato Salad with Basil Mayonnaise; Potato Fattoush.*
*RIGHT: Tri-Fries with Chilli Salt.*

*Bowl from House in Newtown*

# Potatoes

## ROASTED TINY NEW POTATOES WITH AIOLI

**800g tiny new potatoes, unpeeled**
**2 tablespoons olive oil**
**1 large bulb garlic, unpeeled**
**2 tablespoons lemon juice**
**2 egg yolks**
**3/4 cup (180ml) olive oil, extra**
**2 tablespoons shredded fresh**
**    flat-leaf parsley**

Combine potatoes and oil in baking dish; wrap whole garlic bulb in double thickness of foil. Bake potatoes and garlic, uncovered, in moderately hot oven about 45 minutes or until potatoes and garlic are tender. Turn potatoes once, halfway during cooking time.

Separate garlic cloves. Remove and discard skins from 8 garlic cloves; keep remaining garlic and potatoes warm.

Blend or process peeled garlic, juice and egg yolks until pureed. With motor operating, gradually pour in extra oil; process until aïoli thickens. Stir parsley into aïoli; serve with potatoes and remaining unpeeled garlic cloves.

Serves 6.

■ Best made just before serving.
■ Freeze: Not suitable.
■ Microwave: Not suitable.

## POTATO AND PESTO MASH

**1 tablespoon shredded fresh**
**    basil leaves**
**2 tablespoons pine nuts, toasted**
**3 cloves garlic, coarsely chopped**
**1/4 cup (35g) sun-dried tomatoes in**
**    oil, drained, coarsely chopped**
**1/4 cup (20g) coarsely grated**
**    parmesan cheese**
**2 tablespoons lemon juice**
**1/4 cup (60ml) olive oil**
**1.5kg sebago potatoes, peeled,**
**    coarsely chopped**
**80g butter**
**1/2 cup (125ml) hot cream**
**1/3 cup (80ml) hot milk**

Blend or process basil, pine nuts, garlic, tomatoes, cheese and juice until pureed. With motor operating, gradually pour in oil; process until pesto is smooth.

Just before serving, boil, steam or microwave potatoes until tender; drain. Transfer warm potatoes to large bowl; mash with combined butter, cream and milk until smooth. Swirl pesto through potato mixture.

Serves 6 to 8.

■ Pesto can be made a day ahead.
■ Storage: Covered, in refrigerator.
■ Freeze: Not suitable.

*Strainer, bowl and chopping board from Accoutrement; salad servers from House In Newtown*

## BOMBAY POTATO MASALA

**1.5kg spunta potatoes**
**20g butter**
**1 large (200g) onion, sliced**
**3 cloves garlic, crushed**
**1 teaspoon yellow mustard seeds**
**3 teaspoons garam masala**
**2 teaspoons ground coriander**
**2 teaspoons ground cumin**
**1/2 teaspoon chilli powder**
**1/4 teaspoon ground turmeric**
**400g can tomatoes,**
**    undrained, crushed**

Cut potatoes into wedges. Boil, steam or microwave potato wedges until just tender; drain.

Heat butter in large pan; cook onion and garlic, stirring, until onion is soft. Add seeds and spices; cook, stirring, until fragrant. Stir in tomatoes; cook, stirring, 2 minutes or until sauce thickens slightly. Add potatoes; gently stir until heated through.

Serves 6 to 8.

■ Best made just before serving.
■ Freeze: Not suitable.

*LEFT: Bombay Potato Masala.*
*OPPOSITE FROM TOP: Roasted*
*Tiny New Potatoes with Aïoli;*
*Potato and Pesto Mash.*

Square dish from Corso De' Fiori; fluted dish from House In Newtown

91

# Potatoes

## GRANDMA GRACE'S POTATO SALAD

**1.5kg kipfler potatoes, unpeeled**
**6 hard-boiled eggs, chopped**
**1 medium (170g) red onion,**
    **finely chopped**
**6 green onions, finely chopped**
**1 cup (180g) finely chopped**
    **drained gherkins**
**2 tablespoons chopped**
    **fresh parsley**
**1 cup (250ml) mayonnaise**
**¼ cup (60ml) lemon juice**
**2 tablespoons white vinegar**
**3 cloves garlic, finely chopped**

Boil, steam or microwave potatoes until tender; drain. When cool enough to handle, peel; cut into 3cm pieces. Gently toss potatoes with eggs, onions, gherkins, parsley and combined remaining ingredients in large bowl.

Serves 6 to 8.

■ Can be made 3 hours ahead.
■ Storage: Covered, in refrigerator.
■ Freeze: Not suitable.

## WARM POTATO SALAD

**10 shallots, finely chopped**
**2 tablespoons extra virgin olive oil**
**2 bacon rashers, finely chopped**
**800g tiny new potatoes,**
    **unpeeled, sliced**
**2 tablespoons balsamic vinegar**
**2 tablespoons chopped**
    **fresh parsley**

Combine shallots and oil in small bowl; stand 30 minutes.

Meanwhile, cook bacon in small oiled pan until crisp; drain on absorbent paper. Boil, steam or microwave potatoes until just tender; drain. Combine potatoes in large bowl with undrained shallots, bacon and vinegar; cover, stand about 10 minutes. Just before serving, stir in parsley.

Serves 4.

■ Best made just before serving.
■ Freeze: Not suitable.

*RIGHT FROM TOP: Grandma Grace's Potato Salad; Warm Potato Salad.*
*OPPOSITE: Crispy Potato Skins with Mash and Chilli Jam.*

### CRISPY POTATO SKINS WITH MASH AND CHILLI JAM

**6 medium sebago
  potatoes, unpeeled**
**1/2 cup (125ml) hot milk**
**50g butter, melted**
**vegetable oil, for deep-frying**

CHILLI JAM
**2 medium (380g) tomatoes, chopped**
**1 tablespoon Worcestershire sauce**
**2 tablespoons water**
**2 tablespoons brown sugar**
**1/4 cup (60ml) sweet chilli sauce**
**1 tablespoon chopped fresh
  coriander leaves**

Scrub potatoes; boil, steam or microwave until tender. Drain.

When cool enough to handle, cut away 5 strips from each potato, cutting about 1cm into the flesh; reserve strips. Mash remaining potato flesh with combined milk and butter until smooth; cover to keep warm.

Heat oil in large pan; deep-fry potato-skin strips, in batches, in hot oil until browned and crisp. Drain on absorbent paper. Serve immediately with potato mash and Chilli Jam.

**Chilli Jam:** Combine all ingredients in medium pan; stir over low heat until sugar dissolves. Bring to boil; simmer, uncovered, about 15 minutes or until jam thickens and is reduced to about 2/3 cup (160ml). Remove from heat; cool slightly, stir in coriander.

Serves 6.

■ Chilli Jam can be made
  2 days ahead.
■ Storage: Covered, in refrigerator.
■ Freeze: Not suitable.

# Pumpkins

*Belonging to the same gourd family as zucchini and
chokoes, pumpkin was domesticated by natives of the New
World, introduced to Europe by the colonists... and
embraced warmly by us, achieving local hero status with
its appearance in our most popular soup, sweet scones,
and one of the triumvirate surrounding the family roast.*

Tiles from Country Floors

**COOKING METHODS** *Cooking
times are based on 500g pumpkin,
peeled, seeded, chopped.*

**BOIL** *Add pumpkin to large pan
of boiling water; boil, uncovered, about
8 minutes or until tender. Drain.*

**STEAM** *Place pumpkin in
steamer basket; cook, covered, over pan
of simmering water about 20 minutes
or until tender. Drain.*

**MICROWAVE** *Place pumpkin
and 1 tablespoon water in large
microwave-safe dish. Cover, microwave
on HIGH (100%) about 5 minutes or
until tender, pausing halfway during
cooking time to stir. Drain.*

Tested in an 830-watt oven

*Butternut: Small and pear-shaped
with bright-orange flesh. Has a
sweet, nutty flavour complementary
to many vegetable
dishes.*

## ROASTED PUMPKIN MASH

**2kg butternut pumpkin, chopped**
**2 tablespoons olive oil**
**¼ cup (60ml) buttermilk**
**½ cup (40g) finely grated**
   **parmesan cheese**
**60g butter, chopped**
**¼ teaspoon ground nutmeg**

Combine pumpkin and oil in baking dish; bake, uncovered, in very hot oven about 1 hour or until pumpkin is tender and browned lightly.

Transfer pumpkin to large bowl. Working quickly, mash pumpkin then push through fine sieve back into same bowl. Stir in remaining ingredients and serve immediately.

Serves 4 to 6.

■ Best made just before serving.
■ Freeze: Not suitable.
■ Microwave: Not suitable.

*Bowl from Gempo; tiles from Country Floors*

*Jap: Also called Hokkaido. Large, glossy, dark-green with pale yellow speckles and deep yellow flesh; has a pleasant sweet flavour.*

## PUMPKIN CURRY

**2 tablespoons vegetable oil**
**1 large (200g) onion, sliced**
**3 cloves garlic, crushed**
**2 teaspoons grated fresh ginger**
**¾ teaspoon hot chilli powder**
**½ teaspoon ground turmeric**
**2 teaspoons ground cumin**
**2 teaspoons ground coriander**
**1 teaspoon garam masala**
**4 cardamom pods, crushed**
**4 curry leaves, torn**
**1.5kg jap pumpkln, chopped**
**1 cup (250ml) coconut cream**
**½ cup (125ml) water**

Heat oil in medium pan; cook onion, garlic and ginger, stirring, until onion is soft. Add spices, pods and leaves; cook, stirring, about 2 minutes or until fragrant.

Add pumpkin, cream and water; bring to boil, simmer, covered, 10 minutes. Uncover; simmer 10 minutes or until sauce thickens and pumpkin is tender.

Serves 4 to 6.

■ Can be made a day ahead.
■ Storage: Covered, in refrigerator.
■ Freeze: Not suitable.
■ Microwave: Suitable.

*OPPOSITE: Pumpkin Curry.*
*ABOVE: Roasted Pumpkin Mash.*

## GRATED PUMPKIN SALAD

**600g Queensland blue
  pumpkin, coarsely grated**
**¼ cup chopped fresh
  coriander leaves**
**1 tablespoon black mustard seeds**

SOY LIME DRESSING
**⅓ cup (80ml) vegetable oil**
**1 tablespoon soy sauce**
**3 teaspoons lime juice**
**1 tablespoon brown sugar**
**½ teaspoon ground cumin**

Combine pumpkin, leaves, seeds and
three-quarters of the Soy Lime Dressing.
Cover; refrigerate at least 30 minutes.
Just before serving, drizzle remaining
dressing over salad.
**Soy Lime Dressing:** Combine all
ingredients in jar; shake well.

Serves 4.

■ Best made on day of serving.
■ Storage: Covered, in refrigerator.
■ Freeze: Not suitable.

## PUMPKIN PRIMAVERA SALAD

**250g asparagus**
**2 golden nugget pumpkins, sliced**
**250g cherry tomatoes, halved**
**250g teardrop tomatoes, halved**
**¼ cup (20g) parmesan cheese flakes**

ITALIAN DRESSING
**½ cup (125ml) olive oil**
**2 tablespoons coarsely chopped
  fresh basil leaves**
**1 tablespoon white wine vinegar**
**1 clove garlic, coarsely chopped**

Snap off and discard woody ends from
asparagus; cut asparagus into 6cm
lengths. Boil, steam or microwave
asparagus until just tender; rinse under
cold water. Pat dry with absorbent paper.

Boil, steam or microwave pumpkin
until just tender; rinse under cold water.
Pat dry with absorbent paper. Grill or
barbecue pumpkin, in batches, until
browned and tender.

Just before serving, gently mix
pumpkin, tomatoes and asparagus with
Italian Dressing in large bowl; scatter
flaked parmesan over salad.
**Italian Dressing:** Blend or process all
ingredients until smooth.

Serves 4.

■ Italian Dressing can be made
  a day ahead.
■ Storage: Covered, in refrigerator.
■ Freeze: Not suitable.

*LEFT FROM TOP: Grated Pumpkin Salad;
Pumpkin Primavera Salad.*

*Queensland Blue: Perhaps the
best known of all Australian
pumpkins, this large, pale grey-
blue, ridged variety is usually
sold in pre-cut wedges;
good all-round
performer.*

*Nugget: Also called Golden Nugget. Very
small, round, orange skin and dark yellow
flesh; great baked filled with a seasoning.*

97

# Radicchio

*A member of the chicory family, radicchio – along with rocket – is a common Italian salad green (the fact that it's a deep ruby-red in colour notwithstanding). Its ingenious versatility comes into play when you discover that dramatic-looking radicchio, unlike other salad leaves, is just as good grilled or fried as it is eaten raw.*

*Fork from Home & Garden on the Mall*

## CHAR-GRILLED RADICCHIO PARCELS

*Radicchio made its first appearance on most of our tables about the same time as did prosciutto, sun-dried tomatoes and bocconcini: this recipe combines the four in one sensational package.*

**¼ cup (60ml) olive oil**
**75g sliced prosciutto, chopped**
**1 medium (150g) onion, chopped**
**2 cloves garlic, crushed**
**¼ cup (35g) drained sun-dried**
 **tomatoes in oil, chopped**
**200g bocconcini cheese, chopped**
**2 teaspoons drained**
 **capers, chopped**
**2 tablespoons chopped**
 **fresh basil leaves**
**6 large radicchio leaves**
**2 tablespoons olive oil**

Heat 1 tablespoon of the oil in medium pan; cook prosciutto, onion and garlic, stirring, until onion is soft and browned lightly, cool. Combine prosciutto mixture with tomatoes, bocconcini, capers and basil in medium bowl.

Boil, steam or microwave radicchio leaves briefly, until they are just limp; rinse leaves under cold water, pat dry with absorbent paper.

Place leaves on bench. Divide filling mixture among leaves; roll up, folding in edges to enclose filling. Brush parcels all over with some of the remaining oil; cook in heated griddle pan or barbecue until browned and heated through, turning once during cooking. Serve drizzled with any remaining oil.

Serves 6.

- Filling can be made a day ahead.
- Storage: Covered, in refrigerator.
- Freeze: Not suitable.
- Microwave: Radicchio suitable.

*Radicchio*

*LEFT: Char-Grilled Radicchio Parcels.*
*OPPOSITE: Pancetta Radicchio Salad with Anchovy Mayonnaise.*

## PANCETTA RADICCHIO SALAD WITH ANCHOVY MAYONNAISE

*Use a tightly furled, medium-size head of radicchio with a weight in the vicinity of 250g for this recipe.*

**100g sliced pancetta**
**4 eggs**
**1 medium radicchio**
**1 large witlof**
**½ cup (40g) parmesan**
**    cheese flakes**

GARLIC BASIL CROUTONS
**½ small (about 16cm long)**
**    breadstick**
**60g butter, melted**
**1 clove garlic, crushed**
**1 tablespoon finely chopped fresh**
**    basil leaves**

ANCHOVY MAYONNAISE
**1 egg**
**1 tablespoon white wine vinegar**
**1 teaspoon seeded mustard**
**8 drained anchovy fillets**
**¾ cup (180ml) olive oil**
**¼ cup (60ml) buttermilk**

Grill pancetta until crisp and browned; when cool, break into large pieces. Cover eggs with cold water in medium pan; bring to boil then simmer, uncovered, 5 minutes. Drain, shell and halve eggs.

Separate radicchio and witlof leaves; place leaves in bowl. Drizzle with three-quarters of the Anchovy Mayonnaise, then top with pancetta, egg halves, parmesan, Garlic Basil Croutons and, last, the remaining mayonnaise.

**Garlic Basil Croutons:** Cut breadstick into 5mm slices; brush both sides of slices with combined butter, garlic and basil. Place in single layer on oven tray; bake in moderately hot oven for about 8 minutes or until browned and crisp.

**Anchovy Mayonnaise:** Blend or process egg, vinegar, mustard and anchovies until pureed. With motor operating, gradually pour in oil in thin stream; process until thick. Pour in buttermilk; process until combined.

Serves 6 to 8.

■ Garlic Basil Croutons and
    Anchovy Mayonnaise can be made
    a day ahead.
■ Storage: Croutons, in airtight
    container. Mayonnaise, covered, in
    refrigerator.
■ Freeze: Not suitable.
■ Microwave: Not suitable.

## DAIKON AND PICKLED GINGER STIR-FRY

*An everyday fixture at the Japanese table, we are now just starting to experience the wonderful flavour of this long, white radish.*

**1 large (800g) daikon**
**1/2 x 90g packet pickled ginger, drained**
**1 tablespoon peanut oil**
**2 green onions, finely sliced**
**1 1/2 tablespoons mirin**
**1 1/2 tablespoons rice vinegar**
**1 teaspoon wasabi paste**
**2 teaspoons soy sauce**

Peel, top and tail daikon, cut into paper-thin 6cm-long strips. Rinse ginger under cold water; drain, chop roughly. Heat oil in wok or large pan; stir-fry daikon about 5 minutes or until just tender. Add ginger and onions; stir-fry 1 minute. Transfer daikon mixture to serving bowl; drizzle with combined remaining ingredients.

Serves 4 to 6.

■ Best made just before serving.
■ Freeze: Not suitable.
■ Microwave: Not suitable.

## MOROCCAN RADISH AND ORANGE SALAD

*The best way to get the symmetrically paper-thin slices of radish required for this recipe is by using a V-slicer [see Glossary] or mandoline.*

**500g radishes, finely sliced**
**3 large (900g) oranges, segmented**
**1/3 cup (50g) shelled pistachios, toasted**
**1/4 cup chopped fresh chives**
**2 teaspoons sumac [see Glossary]**
**1/4 cup (60ml) orange juice**
**2 tablespoons olive oil**
**1 tablespoon lemon juice**
**1 teaspoon sugar**
**1/2 teaspoon ground cumin**
**1 teaspoon white wine vinegar**
**1 clove garlic, crushed**

*Daikon Radish*

Combine radish slices, oranges, nuts, chives and sumac in large bowl; pour combined remaining ingredients over salad mixture. Toss salad gently; cover, refrigerate at least 1 hour before serving.

Serves 6.

■ Can be made 3 hours ahead.
■ Storage: Covered, in refrigerator.
■ Freeze: Not suitable.

*ABOVE: Daikon and Pickled Ginger Stir-Fry.*
*OPPOSITE: Moroccan Radish and Orange Salad.*

*White Radish*

*Radish*

# Radish

*When you were a child, what was summer without a*
*peppery radish and buttered white bread sandwich?*
*Round or elongated, red or white – but always piquant,*
*crunchy and clean-tasting – radishes warrant a closer*
*look than being just one of a crowded platter of crudités.*

Setting from Opus

# Rocket

*Arugula, rocket, roquette, rucola, rugula – call it what you will, but this distinctive salad green will always answer back with spicy assertiveness. Rocket has launched onto today's table in a big way, and no wonder: whether used in cooking or served raw flaked with parmesan and drizzled with balsamic vinegar, it's a blast.*

Rocket

*Bowl from Much Ado Gallery; napkin from Orson & Blake Collectables*

### ROCKET SALAD WITH TOMATO VINAIGRETTE

30g butter
2 cloves garlic, crushed
50g pastrami, chopped
2 teaspoons brown sugar
2 cups (140g) stale sourdough
   breadcrumbs
2 tablespoons chopped fresh
   coriander leaves
250g rocket

TOMATO VINAIGRETTE
3 small (390g) tomatoes
1/4 cup (60ml) white wine vinegar
2 teaspoons Worcestershire sauce
few drops Tabasco sauce
1 teaspoon sugar
1/3 cup (80ml) olive oil

Heat butter in large pan; cook garlic and pastrami, stirring, until pastrami is crisp. Stir in sugar and breadcrumbs; cook, stirring, until breadcrumbs are browned. Remove from heat; stir in coriander.

Just before serving, toss rocket in Tomato Vinaigrette in large bowl; sprinkle with breadcrumb mixture.

**Tomato Vinaigrette:** Blend or process tomatoes, vinegar, sauces and sugar until pureed. With motor operating, gradually pour in oil; process until smooth. Strain into jug.

Serves 6.

- ◼ Salad must be made just before serving. Breadcrumbs and Tomato Vinaigrette can be made a day ahead.
- ◼ Storage: Breadcrumbs in an airtight container. Vinaigrette, covered, in refrigerator.
- ◼ Freeze: Not suitable.
- ◼ Microwave: Not suitable.

## ROCKET POLENTA WEDGES

**60g butter**
**1 small (200g) leek, finely chopped**
**2 cloves garlic, crushed**
**1/3 cup (50g) plain flour**
**2 tablespoons polenta**
**1 cup (250ml) milk**
**4 eggs, separated**
**1/2 cup (40g) coarsely grated parmesan cheese**
**125g rocket, chopped**

Oil 19cm x 29cm rectangular slice pan; line with baking paper, extending paper 2cm over edge of long sides of pan.

Heat butter in medium pan; cook leek and garlic, stirring, until leek is soft. Stir in flour and polenta gradually; cook, stirring, 1 minute. Remove from heat; gradually stir in milk. Return to heat; cook, stirring, until mixture boils and thickens. Remove from heat; stir in lightly beaten egg yolks, parmesan and rocket. Transfer mixture to large bowl.

Beat egg whites in small bowl with electric mixer until soft peaks form; fold into rocket polenta mixture in 2 batches. Spread mixture into prepared pan; bake, uncovered, in hot oven about 12 minutes or until browned. Turn onto board; cut into wedges.

Serves 6.

- ◼ Best made just before serving.
- ◼ Freeze: Not suitable.
- ◼ Microwave: Not suitable.

*OPPOSITE: Rocket Salad with Tomato Vinaigrette.*
*ABOVE: Rocket Polenta Wedges.*

# Silverbeet

*Silverbeet can be labelled spinach, seakale, blettes or Swiss chard, depending on which part of the world you find it in. A hard-working vegetable, both silverbeet's sturdy dark-green leaf and thick white stem, used together or separately, can be presented in a plethora of different ways, not least of which is dressed simply in your favourite vinaigrette.*

**COOKING METHODS** *Cooking times are based on 500g silverbeet, white stems cut off and discarded, leaves washed thoroughly.*

**BOIL** *Add whole leaves to large pan of boiling water; boil, uncovered, about 2 minutes or until tender. Drain.*

**STEAM** *Place chopped leaves in steamer basket; cook, covered, over pan of simmering water about 4 minutes or until tender. Drain.*

**MICROWAVE** *Place whole leaves in large microwave-safe dish. Cover, microwave on HIGH (100%) about 4 minutes or until tender, pausing halfway during cooking time to stir. Drain.*

Tested in an 850-watt oven

*Silverbeet*

*LEFT FROM TOP: Silverbeet Dhal; Silverbeet and Potato Mash. OPPOSITE: Baby Silverbeet with Raspberry Vinaigrette.*

### SILVERBEET DHAL

1 cup (200g) red lentils
1 large (200g) onion
2 tablespoons ghee
3 cloves garlic, crushed
1 tablespoon grated fresh ginger
1 tablespoon Madras curry paste
400g can tomatoes,
    undrained, crushed
1/2 cup (125ml) vegetable stock
500g silverbeet, stems discarded,
    leaves chopped
1 tablespoon lemon juice

Wash lentils under cold water; drain. Cut onion in half lengthways then into wedges. Heat ghee in large pan; cook onion, garlic and ginger, stirring, about 5 minutes or until onion is soft. Add curry paste; cook, stirring, about 2 minutes or until fragrant. Stir in lentils, tomatoes and stock; simmer, covered, over low heat for about 30 minutes or until lentils are tender, stirring occasionally. Add the silverbeet; cook, stirring, until silverbeet is just wilted. Stir in lemon juice.

Serves 4 to 6.

■ Best made just before serving.
■ Freeze: Not suitable.
■ Microwave: Not suitable.

### SILVERBEET AND POTATO MASH

*Buy the best mashing potato you can find for this recipe — try using Spunta, King Edward or Sebago potatoes [see Potatoes] if they're available.*

1kg potatoes, chopped
60g butter
1 small (80g) onion, chopped
8 anchovy fillets
1/2 cup (125ml) milk
1kg silverbeet, stems discarded,
    leaves finely shredded
2 tablespoons cream

Boil, steam or microwave potatoes until tender; drain. Push potatoes through coarse sieve into large bowl; cover to keep warm. Heat butter in medium pan; cook onion and anchovies, stirring, until onion is soft and anchovies break up. Stir onion mixture and warmed milk into potatoes in serving bowl; cover.

Boil, steam or microwave silverbeet until just wilted; drain. Squeeze out excess liquid from silverbeet; combine with cream in medium bowl. Gently swirl silverbeet mixture through potato mixture.

Serves 4 to 6.

■ Best made just before serving.
■ Freeze: Not suitable.

### BABY SILVERBEET WITH RASPBERRY VINAIGRETTE

*You can substitute frozen raspberries, thawed and well-drained, if fresh ones aren't available.*

150g baby silverbeet leaves
50g mesclun [see Lettuce]
1/2 cup (75g) fresh raspberries
1/3 cup (35g) chopped
    hazelnuts, toasted
1 small (100g) red onion,
    thinly sliced
RASPBERRY VINAIGRETTE
1/2 cup (75g) fresh raspberries
1/3 cup (80ml) orange juice
1 tablespoon hazelnut oil
1 tablespoon vegetable oil
1 teaspoon sugar

Gently toss all salad ingredients with Raspberry Vinaigrette in medium bowl.
**Raspberry Vinaigrette:** Blend or process all ingredients until smooth; strain into jug.

Serves 4.

■ Salad must be made just before serving. Raspberry Vinaigrette can be made a day ahead.
■ Storage: Covered, in refrigerator.
■ Freeze: Not suitable.

# Spinach

*Spinach is a world away, in looks and taste, from the leafy, green silverbeet, with which it is often confused. While sometimes called English spinach, it was first cultivated in the Middle-East, taken to Spain and thence to America where it was popularised by Popeye! What a lineage! What an aristocrat of vegetables!*

**COOKING METHODS** *Cooking times are based on 1 bunch (500g) English spinach, roots and about 6cm of lower stems cut off and discarded, leaves washed thoroughly.*

**BOIL** *Add spinach to large pan of boiling water; remove immediately, refresh under cold water. Drain well.*

**STEAM** *Place spinach in steamer basket; cook, covered, over pan of simmering water about 3 minutes or until just wilted, tossing halfway through cooking time. Drain.*

**MICROWAVE** *Place spinach in large microwave-safe bowl. Cover, microwave on HIGH (100%) about 3 minutes or until just wilted; refresh under cold water. Drain well.*

Tested in an 850-watt oven

## GARLICKY ONIONY SPINACH

*Dried onion flakes are available from most supermarkets.*

**1 tablespoon vegetable oil**
**5 cloves garlic, thinly sliced**
**2 bunches (1kg) spinach (trimmed as described at left)**
**2 teaspoons cornflour**
**1/2 cup (125ml) chicken stock**
**2 teaspoons soy sauce**
**2 tablespoons onion flakes, toasted**

Heat oil in wok or large pan; cook garlic, stirring, until it starts to brown. Add spinach and blended corn- flour, stock and sauce; cook, stirring, until spinach is just wilted and sauce boils and thickens slightly. Sprinkle with toasted onion flakes.

Serves 4 to 6.

■ Best made just before serving.
■ Freeze: Not suitable.
■ Microwave: Not suitable.

*English Spinach*

Bowl, plate and tray from Made in Japan; spoon from The Bay Tree Kitchen Shop

# Spinach

## CREAMED SPINACH

*We used creme fraiche here, but light sour cream can be substituted.*

**20g butter**
**2 bunches (1kg) spinach (trimmed as described on previous page)**
**1 tablespoon olive oil**
**1 large (200g) onion, chopped**
**5 slices (75g) prosciutto, chopped**
**2 cloves garlic, crushed**
**200ml creme fraiche**
**1/4 cup chopped fresh chives**
**1/4 teaspoon ground nutmeg**

Heat butter in large pan; cook spinach, covered, stirring occasionally, until just wilted. Drain; gently squeeze spinach to remove excess liquid.

Heat oil in same pan; cook onion, prosciutto and garlic, stirring, until the prosciutto is browned and crisp. Add spinach and remaining ingredients; cook, stirring, until heated through.

Serves 6.

■ Best made just before serving.
■ Freeze: Not suitable.
■ Microwave: Not suitable.

*Plate from Waterford Wedgwood; tiles from Country Floors*

## SPINACH SALAD WITH TOFFEE PECANS AND BLUE CHEESE

1/4 cup (55g) sugar
1/2 cup (50g) pecans
160g baby spinach leaves
1/2 cup (125ml) olive oil
2 tablespoons white wine vinegar
1/2 teaspoon sugar
80g creamy blue-vein cheese
1 clove garlic, crushed

Heat sugar in shallow pan, without stirring, until golden brown; mix nuts with sugar in pan until well coated. Transfer nut mixture to oiled oven tray; cool then chop roughly.

Just before serving, gently toss toffee pecans and spinach with combined remaining ingredients.

Serves 4 to 6.

■ Toffee Pecans can be made a day ahead.
■ Storage: In airtight container.
■ Freeze: Not suitable.
■ Microwave: Not suitable.

## SPINACH CAESAR SALAD

6 bacon rashers, chopped
1/2 loaf unsliced white bread
1 tablespoon olive oil
375g baby spinach leaves
4 eggs, hard-boiled, quartered
2 tablespoons chopped fresh chives
1/3 cup (25g) parmesan cheese flakes

SPINACH DRESSING
125g baby spinach leaves
1 egg yolk
1 tablespoon white wine vinegar
1 clove garlic, crushed
3 anchovy fillets
2 teaspoons Dijon mustard
1/2 teaspoon sugar
3 teaspoons lemon juice
1/3 cup (80ml) vegetable oil
1/4 cup (60ml) buttermilk

Cook bacon in heated dry pan, stirring, until crisp; drain on absorbent paper.

Remove breadcrust; cut bread lengthways into 2cm slices. Using a 3cm cutter, cut bread into shapes; toss shapes and oil in medium bowl, place on oven tray. Bake in moderate oven about 10 minutes or until browned lightly, turning once.

Gently toss spinach, bacon, bread shapes, eggs, chives and half the cheese in a large bowl. Arrange salad on serving platter; drizzle with Spinach Dressing, sprinkle with remaining cheese.

**Spinach Dressing:** Boil, steam or microwave spinach until just wilted; cool. Squeeze out excess moisture; roughly chop spinach. Blend or process egg yolk, vinegar, garlic, anchovies, mustard, sugar and juice until pureed. With motor operating, gradually pour in oil; process until thick. Add buttermilk and spinach; process until smooth.

Serves 6.

■ Best made just before serving.
■ Freeze: Not suitable.

*OPPOSITE ABOVE: Creamed Spinach.*
*OPPOSITE BELOW: Spinach Salad with Toffee Pecans and Blue Cheese.*
*BELOW: Spinach Caesar Salad.*

## SWEDE AND KUMARA BAKE

**500g swedes, sliced**
**250g kumara, sliced**
**1 medium (150g) onion, sliced**
**3/4 cup (90g) grated cheddar cheese**
**1/4 cup (20g) grated**
    **parmesan cheese**
**2 tablespoons chopped fresh dill**
**2 teaspoons cracked black pepper**
**1/2 cup (125ml) cream**

Oil 2.5-litre (10-cup) shallow ovenproof dish. Layer half of the swede, kumara and onion in prepared dish; sprinkle with half of the combined cheeses, dill and pepper. Repeat with remaining swede, kumara and onion. Pour cream over top of vegetables; top with remaining cheese mixture. Bake, covered, in moderate oven 1 hour; uncover, bake about 30 minutes or until top is browned and vegetables are tender.

Serves 6.

■ Can be made a day ahead.
■ Storage: Covered, in refrigerator.
■ Freeze: Not suitable.
■ Microwave: Not suitable.

## SPICED MASHED SWEDE

**1/4 cup (35g) currants**
**1/4 cup (60ml) orange juice**
**1kg swedes, chopped**
**2 teaspoons peanut oil**
**1 medium (150g) onion, chopped**
**2 cloves garlic, crushed**
**2 teaspoons ground cumin**
**2 teaspoons ground coriander**
**2 tablespoons chopped fresh**
    **coriander leaves**

Combine currants and juice in small bowl; stand 30 minutes. Drain; discard juice. Boil, steam or microwave swedes until tender; drain. Mash with potato masher in large bowl; keep warm.

Heat oil in small pan; cook onion, garlic and ground spices, stirring, until onion is soft. Combine onion mixture, currants and coriander with mashed swede.

Serves 4.

■ Best made just before serving.
■ Freeze: Not suitable.
■ Microwave: Suitable.

*ABOVE LEFT: Swede and Kumara Bake.*
*LEFT: Spiced Mashed Swede.*
*OPPOSITE: Hazelnut-Coated Swede and Beetroot Croquettes.*

*Setting from House In Newtown*

# Swedes

*The swede is also known as a rutabaga, a bastardisation of an archaic Swedish word, rotabaggee. Sometimes confused with the turnip, the swede is in fact a member of the cabbage family, and is eaten throughout winter in northern Europe, especially Scotland where, mashed with potatoes, it becomes tatties and neeps, traditionally accompanying haggis.*

**COOKING METHODS** *Cooking times are based on 4 medium (500g) swedes, peeled, chopped into 3cm pieces.*

**BOIL** *Add swedes to large pan of boiling water; boil, uncovered, about 15 minutes or until tender. Drain.*

**STEAM** *Place swedes in steamer basket; cook, uncovered, over pan of boiling water about 20 minutes or until tender. Drain.*

**MICROWAVE** *Place swedes in large microwave-safe dish. Cover, microwave on HIGH (100%) about 8 minutes or until tender, pausing halfway during cooking time to stir. Drain.*

Tested in an 830-watt oven

## HAZELNUT-COATED SWEDE AND BEETROOT CROQUETTES

**1kg swedes, roughly chopped**
**1 medium (160g) beetroot**
**1 tablespoon olive oil**
**2 cloves garlic, crushed**
**1 medium onion, finely chopped**
**1/2 cup (75g) plain flour**
**3 eggs, lightly beaten**
**1/2 cup (125ml) milk**
**1 1/4 cups (85g) stale breadcrumbs**
**3/4 cup (110g) hazelnuts, finely chopped**
**vegetable oil, for deep-frying**

Boil, steam or microwave swedes and beetroot, separately, until tender; drain. Combine swedes and beetroot; mash in large bowl. Cool.

Heat oil in small pan; cook garlic and onion, stirring, until onion is soft. Stir garlic and onion into vegetable mash. When mixture is cool, shape 2 tablespoons of mixture into croquette; place on foil-lined tray. Repeat with remaining mixture; refrigerate about 30 minutes or until croquettes are firm.

Roll croquettes in flour, shake away excess; dip in combined eggs and milk, then combined breadcrumbs and nuts. Just before serving, deep-fry croquettes in hot oil until golden brown; drain on absorbent paper.

Makes 18.

■ Uncooked croquettes can be made a day ahead.
■ Store: Covered, in refrigerator.
■ Freeze: Suitable.

*Swede*

111

**Cherry**

**Egg**

# Tomatoes

**Vine-Ripened**

**Teardrop**

*You say tomaytoes while I say tomahtoes, but we nevertheless agree on the so-called love apple's qualities: amazing versatility, fabulous flavour and loaded with vitamins. Another food that originated in the New World, tomato seeds were taken to Europe by the Spaniards... and Mediterranean cooking never looked back.*

## TOMATO BRUSCHETTA SALAD

½ loaf (12cm x 18cm) Italian bread
¼ cup (60ml) olive oil
3 medium (570g) tomatoes,
    roughly chopped
1 large (300g) red onion,
    roughly chopped
125g rocket, torn
1 cup (80g) parmesan cheese flakes
⅓ cup shredded fresh basil leaves
⅓ cup (80ml) olive oil
2 tablespoons red wine vinegar
1 clove garlic, crushed
1 teaspoon sugar

Cut bread into 4cm pieces. Heat oil in large pan; cook bread pieces, stirring, until browned and crisp, drain on absorbent paper.

Just before serving, gently toss warm bread, tomatoes, onion, rocket, parmesan and basil with combined remaining ingredients in large bowl.

Serves 6.

■ Best made just before serving.
■ Freeze: Not suitable.
■ Microwave: Not suitable.

## PENNE WITH SAUTEED TOMATOES AND FETTA

250g penne pasta
¼ cup (60ml) olive oil
2 medium (300g) onions, sliced
2 cloves garlic, crushed
2 tablespoons pine nuts
250g cherry tomatoes
250g teardrop tomatoes
1 teaspoon cracked black pepper
350g fetta cheese, chopped
1 tablespoon chopped
    fresh oregano

Add pasta to large pan of boiling water. Boil, uncovered, until just tender; drain.

Heat oil in large pan; cook onions, garlic and nuts, stirring, until onions are soft and nuts browned. Add both tomatoes and pepper; cook, stirring, until tomatoes just begin to soften. Stir in pasta, fetta and oregano until mixture is heated through and cheese softens.

Serves 6.

■ Best made just before serving.
■ Freeze: Not suitable.
■ Microwave: Not suitable.

## ROASTED TOMATOES WITH BALSAMIC DRESSING

12 large (1kg) egg tomatoes,
    halved lengthways
½ cup (125ml) olive oil
1 tablespoon sugar
2 cloves garlic, crushed
1 teaspoon salt
1 teaspoon cracked black pepper
1 tablespoon balsamic vinegar
1 tablespoon shredded fresh
    basil leaves

Place tomatoes, cut side up, on wire rack in baking dish. Brush with half of the combined oil, sugar, garlic, salt and pepper. Bake, uncovered, in moderate oven about 1½ hours or until tomatoes are softened and browned lightly.

Drizzle combined remaining oil and vinegar over tomatoes; scatter with basil.

Serves 6.

■ Can be made 3 days ahead.
■ Storage: Covered, in refrigerator.
■ Freeze: Not suitable.
■ Microwave: Not suitable.

*OPPOSITE FROM TOP: Tomato Bruschetta Salad; Penne with Sauteed Tomatoes and Fetta.*
*ABOVE: Roasted Tomatoes with Balsamic Dressing.*

**COOKING METHODS** *Cooking times are based on 4 medium (500g) turnips, thickly peeled, roughly chopped. (Thickly peeling turnips removes the slightly bitter taste they sometimes have.)*

**BOIL** *Add turnips to large pan of boiling water; boil, uncovered, about 9 minutes or until tender. Drain.*

**STEAM** *Place turnips in steamer basket; cook, covered, over pan of simmering water about 12 minutes or until tender. Drain.*

**MICROWAVE** *Place turnips and 1 tablespoon water in large microwave-safe dish. Cover, microwave on HIGH (100%) about 6 minutes or until tender, pausing halfway during cooking time to stir. Drain.*

Tested in an 850-watt oven

## CREAMY TURNIP MASH

*If small baby turnips are available, use them in this recipe for their delicate, sweet flavour.*

**600g turnips, chopped**
**5 medium (1kg) potatoes, chopped**
**200ml creme fraiche**
**⅓ cup (25g) grated parmesan cheese**

CARAMELISED ONIONS
**50g butter**
**2 medium (300g) onions, finely sliced**
**2 tablespoons sugar**
**1 tablespoon brown malt vinegar**

Boil, steam or microwave turnips and potatoes, separately, until tender; drain. Combine vegetables; mash with creme fraiche and parmesan in large bowl. Stir Caramelised Onions through mash.
**Caramelised Onions:** Heat butter in medium pan; cook onions, stirring, about 10 minutes or until soft. Add sugar and vinegar; stir over heat about 10 minutes or until onions are caramelised.

Serves 6.

■ Best made just before serving.
■ Freeze: Not suitable.
■ Microwave: Onions not suitable.

*Tiles from Country Floors*

*Turnip*

# Turnips

*The homely turnip's sweet bitterness marries so well with traditional meat dishes that it can easily displace a potato. Plus, it's been re-invented to gain contemporary cachet by scenting a Moroccan stew, masquerading in a mash or nestling in a bunch of purple-tinged miniatures.*

## ROASTED TURNIPS

**1kg turnips, roughly chopped**
**8 cloves garlic, unpeeled**
**1 tablespoon brown sugar**
**2 tablespoons olive oil**
**1 teaspoon cumin seeds**

Toss turnips and garlic with combined remaining ingredients in large bowl. Place in baking dish; bake, uncovered, in moderately hot oven for about 30 minutes or until browned lightly, stirring occasionally.

Serves 4 to 6.

■ Best made just before serving.
■ Freeze: Not suitable.
■ Microwave: Not suitable.

## TURNIP RATATOUILLE

**2 medium (600g) eggplants**
**¼ cup (60ml) olive oil**
**2 cloves garlic, crushed**
**1kg turnips, roughly chopped**
**2 small (300g) red capsicums, roughly chopped**
**2 medium (240g) green zucchini, chopped**
**2 large (300g) yellow zucchini, chopped**
**2 x 400g cans tomatoes, undrained, crushed**
**2 tablespoons tomato paste**
**1 tablespoon capers, rinsed, drained, chopped**
**2 tablespoons dry red wine**
**¼ cup firmly packed basil leaves, shredded**

Cut eggplants into 1cm slices; quarter slices. Heat oil in large heavy-based pan; cook eggplant and garlic, stirring, about 5 minutes or until just tender and browned lightly. Add turnips, capsicum, zucchini, tomatoes, paste, capers and wine; simmer, covered, about 30 minutes or until vegetables are tender. Stir in half the basil; sprinkle remaining half over top of ratatouille just before serving.

Serves 8.

■ Can be made a day ahead.
■ Storage: Covered, in refrigerator.
■ Freeze: Not suitable.
■ Microwave: Not suitable.

*Dishes from Opus; tiles from Country Floors*

*OPPOSITE: Creamy Turnip Mash.*
*ABOVE FROM TOP: Roasted Turnips; Turnip Ratatouille.*

# Witlof

*Grown in the dark to retain its pale colour and singular bittersweet taste, elegant witlof – also known as witloof, Belgium endive or even chicory – creates a frisson of flavour once exposed to the light of the myriad delicious ways it can be eaten, raw or cooked.*

China from Villeroy & Boch

### WITLOF AU GRATIN

6 medium (750g) witlof
60g butter, chopped
1 tablespoon brown sugar
½ teaspoon cracked black pepper
½ teaspoon fine sea salt
2 tablespoons plain flour
1⅓ cups (330ml) milk
⅓ cup (80ml) cream
⅓ cup (25g) finely grated
   parmesan cheese
2 teaspoons packaged breadcrumbs

*Witlof*

Place witlof in 1.5-litre (6-cup) shallow ovenproof dish; dot witlof with half the butter, sprinkle with sugar, pepper and salt. Bake, covered, in moderate oven, 1½ hours. Uncover; bake 20 minutes or until witlof are soft. Drain and discard juices from dish.

Meanwhile, heat remaining butter in small pan. Stir in flour; cook, stirring, until bubbling. Remove from heat, gradually stir in milk; stir over heat until mixture boils and thickens. Stir in cream and half the parmesan. Pour sauce over witlof; sprinkle with combined remaining parmesan and breadcrumbs. Bake, uncovered, in moderately hot oven about 20 minutes or until browned lightly. Stand 5 minutes before serving.

Serves 6.

■ Best made just before serving.
■ Freeze: Not suitable.
■ Microwave: Sauce suitable.

## WITLOF SALAD
**4 medium (500g) witlof**
**1 tablespoon olive oil**
**3 bacon rashers, finely chopped**
**2 small (400g) leeks, finely sliced**
**3 medium (360g) zucchini, finely sliced**
**310g can corn kernels, rinsed, drained**
**100g mesclun [see Lettuce]**
**¼ cup chopped fresh flat-leaf parsley**
**3 hard-boiled eggs, quartered**

### DIJON DRESSING
**¼ cup (60ml) olive oil**
**2 tablespoons Dijon mustard**
**2 tablespoons lemon juice**
**1 tablespoon mayonnaise**
**1½ teaspoons sugar**
**1 teaspoon balsamic vinegar**

Trim and discard 3cm off each witlof base; separate leaves.

Heat oil in large pan, cook bacon, stirring, 1 minute. Add leeks and zucchini; cook, stirring, about 5 minutes, or until vegetables are tender. Cool.

Gently toss witlof, vegetable mixture, corn, mesclun and parsley with half the dressing in large serving bowl. Place eggs on top of salad; drizzle with remaining dressing.

**Dijon Dressing:** Combine all ingredients in jar; shake well.

Serves 6.

■ Best made just before serving.
■ Freeze: Not suitable.

*OPPOSITE: Witlof Au Gratin.*
*ABOVE: Witlof Salad.*

# Zucchini & Squash

*Known collectively as summer squash (to distinguish them from winter squashes, like pumpkins which have inedible seeds and skins), zucchini, pattipan or pattypan, and marrows can be eaten in their entirety – even their flowers! Available year round, their adaptability and versatility have made them almost as popular here as they are in southern Europe.*

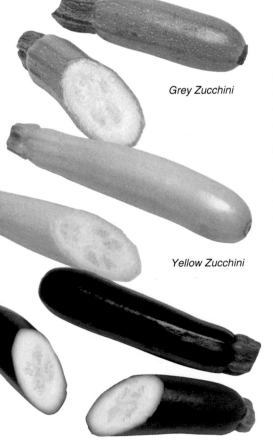

*Grey Zucchini*

*Yellow Zucchini*

*Green Zucchini*

## Zucchini

**COOKING METHODS** *Cooking times are based on 4 medium (500g) zucchini, trimmed, halved crossways.*

**BOIL** *Add zucchini to medium pan of boiling water; boil, uncovered, about 4 minutes or until tender. Drain.*

**STEAM** *Place zucchini in steamer basket; cook, covered, over pan of simmering water about 6 minutes or until tender. Drain.*

**MICROWAVE** *Place zucchini and 2 tablespoons water in medium microwave-safe dish. Cover, microwave on HIGH (100%) about 5 minutes, pausing halfway during cooking time to stir. Drain.*
Tested in an 850-watt oven

## DEEP-FRIED RICOTTA-FILLED ZUCCHINI FLOWERS

*Try growing your own zucchini (or making friends with a farmer) so that you can pick flowers with a new zucchini just forming – the taste is unforgettable.*

**18 zucchini flowers**
**½ cup (75g) plain flour**
**2 tablespoons cornflour**
**2 tablespoons polenta**
**½ teaspoon sugar**
**2 egg whites**
**½ cup (125ml) water**
**vegetable oil, for deep-frying**

RICOTTA FILLING
**1 cup (200g) ricotta cheese**
**2 green onions, finely chopped**
**2 tablespoons pine nuts, toasted**
**1 tablespoon chopped**
   **fresh basil leaves**
**2 cloves garlic, crushed**

Remove and discard flower stamens from centre of flowers; divide Ricotta Filling ingredients among the flowers.

Twist flower petals to enclose filling. Sift flours, polenta and sugar into medium bowl; stir in combined egg whites and water, mix to a smooth batter. Dip flowers in batter to coat completely. Heat oil in large pan; deep-fry flowers, in batches, until browned lightly and crisp. Drain on absorbent paper.
**Ricotta Filling:** Combine all ingredients in small bowl.

Serves 4 to 6.

■ Zucchini Flowers must be made just before serving. Ricotta Filling can be made 3 hours ahead.
■ Storage: Covered, in refrigerator.
■ Freeze: Not suitable.
■ Microwave: Not suitable.

## ZUCCHINI AND TOMATO BAKE

**6 medium (750g) zucchini**
**4 medium (300g) egg tomatoes**
**1 medium (150g) onion**
**3 cloves garlic, crushed**
**¼ cup chopped fresh oregano**
**¼ cup (60ml) olive oil**
**⅓ cup (50g) drained sun-dried**
**    tomatoes in oil, chopped**

Halve each zucchini crossways; quarter
each half lengthways. Quarter tomatoes
lengthways. Halve onion; cut halves into
wedges. Gently toss zucchini, tomato,
onion, garlic and oregano with oil in
large bowl to coat. Place in baking dish;
bake, covered, in hot oven 20 minutes.
Stir in sun-dried tomato pieces; bake,
uncovered, 15 minutes or until zucchini
are just tender.

Serves 6.

■ Best made just before serving.
■ Freeze: Not suitable.
■ Microwave: Not suitable.

## TUNISIAN-STYLE SQUASH WITH COUSCOUS

*Some greengrocers call pattipan*
*squash either acorn squash or*
*scallopini, and they usually come in*
*both a pale green and yellow variety,*
*just like zucchini.*

**3 medium (375g) green zucchini**
**3 medium (375g) yellow zucchini**
**6 medium (200g) green**
**    pattipan squash**
**6 medium (200g) yellow**
**    pattipan squash**
**1 tablespoon ground cumin**
**2 cloves garlic, crushed**
**¼ cup (60ml) hot chilli sauce**
**2 tablespoons olive oil**
**1 cup (200g) couscous**
**1 cup (250ml) boiling water**
**20g butter**

Halve zucchini crossways, then into
slices lengthways; slice squash thinly.
Gently toss zucchini, squash, cumin,
garlic, sauce with oil in large bowl to
coat. Cook vegetables, in batches, in
heated oiled griddle pan (or grill or
barbecue) until browned and tender.

Meanwhile, combine remaining ingredients in heatproof bowl; cover, stand
5 minutes or until water is absorbed.
Fluff couscous with fork before serving
with vegetables.

Serves 4 to 6.

■ Best made just before serving.
■ Freeze: Not suitable.
■ Microwave: Not suitable.

*CLOCKWISE FROM LEFT: Tunisian-Style*
*Squash with Couscous; Zucchini and*
*Tomato Bake; Deep-Fried Ricotta-Filled*
*Zucchini Flowers.*

# Squash

**COOKING METHODS** *Cooking times are based on 500g pattipan squash, trimmed, quartered.*

**BOIL** *Add squash to medium pan of boiling water; boil, uncovered, about 4 minutes or until tender. Drain.*

**STEAM** *Place squash in steamer basket; cook, covered, over pan of simmering water about 6 minutes or until tender. Drain.*

**MICROWAVE** *Place squash and 2 tablespoons water in medium microwave-safe dish. Cover, microwave on HIGH (100%) about 4 minutes, pausing halfway during cooking time to stir. Drain.*

Tested in an 850-watt oven

*Pattipan Squash*

*Zucchini Flowers*

## ZUCCHINI AND RADISH SUMMER SALAD

**6 medium (750g) zucchini**
**250g radishes, thinly sliced**
**4 green onions, chopped**
**1 tablespoon chopped drained pickled ginger**
**2 tablespoons mirin**
**1 tablespoon rice vinegar**
**few drops sesame oil**

Using a V-slicer [see Glossary], cut zucchini into thin strips. Gently toss zucchini, radishes, onions and ginger with combined remaining ingredients in large bowl; mix well.

Serves 4 to 6.

■ Best made just before serving.
■ Freeze: Not suitable.
■ Microwave: Not suitable.

## ZUCCHINI AND CABBAGE STIR-FRY

**40g butter**
**2 cloves garlic, crushed**
**2 small fresh red chillies, chopped**
**6 medium (750g) zucchini,**
    **coarsely grated**
**250g Chinese cabbage,**
    **finely chopped**
**1 tablespoon lemon juice**

Heat butter in wok or large pan; cook garlic and chillies, stirring, until garlic is fragrant. Add remaining ingredients; stir-fry until just cooked and heated through.

Serves 6 to 8.

■ Best made just before serving.
■ Freeze: Not suitable.
■ Microwave: Not suitable.

Bowl from Dinosaur Designs

## ZUCCHINI TIMBALES WITH LIME-BUTTERMILK CREAM

**4 medium (500g) zucchini,**
    **coarsely grated**
**1 medium (150g) apple, unpeeled,**
    **coarsely grated**
**1 tablespoon chopped fresh**
    **mint leaves**
**2 teaspoons lime juice**

LIME-BUTTERMILK CREAM
**1 cup (250ml) buttermilk**
**1/4 cup (60ml) mayonnaise**
**2 teaspoons grated lime rind**
**2 tablespoons lime juice**
**1 teaspoon horseradish cream**
**1 teaspoon sugar**

Oil 4 x 1/2-cup (125ml) moulds, line bases with baking paper. Combine all timbale ingredients in medium bowl; drain mixture in sieve, pressing out as much liquid as possible. Press mixture firmly into prepared moulds; turn onto individual serving plates. Serve with Lime-Buttermilk Cream.
**Lime-Buttermilk Cream:** Combine all ingredients in small bowl; whisk well.

Serves 4.

■ Timbales best made just before serving. Lime-Buttermilk Cream can be made a day ahead.
■ Storage: Covered, in refrigerator.
■ Freeze: Not suitable.
■ Microwave: Not suitable.

Plate from Dinosaur Designs

*OPPOSITE: Zucchini and Radish Summer Salad.*
*ABOVE: Zucchini and Cabbage Stir-Fry.*
*LEFT: Zucchini Timbales with Lime-Buttermilk Cream.*

121

Garam masala

Walnuts

Saffron

Hazelnuts

Thyme

# Glossary

Rosemary

Marjoram

Dill

*Here are some terms, names and alternatives to help everyone use and understand our recipes perfectly.*

Curly Parsley

Coriander

Flat-leaf parsley

Mint

Oregano

Basil

Curry leaves

Lemon grass

**ALLSPICE:** also known as Jamaican pepper or pimento; available whole or ground. Tastes like a blend of cinnamon, clove and nutmeg.

**BACON RASHERS:** also known as slices of bacon; made of cured and smoked pork side.

**BAKING PAPER:** also known as parchment, silicon paper or non-stick baking paper; not to be confused with greaseproof or wax(ed) paper. Used to line pans; can also be used to make piping bags.

**BAKING POWDER:** a raising agent consisting mainly of 2 parts cream of tartar to 1 part bicarbonate of soda (baking soda).

**BARBECUE SAUCE:** a spicy tomato-based sauce used to marinate and baste, or as an accompaniment to roasted or grilled foods.

**BEAN SPROUTS:** also known as bean shoots; tender new growths of assorted beans and seeds germinated for consumption as sprouts. The most readily available are mung bean, soy bean, alfalfa and snow pea sprouts.

**BEETROOT:** also known as beets.

**BICARBONATE OF SODA:** also known as baking soda.

**BISCUITS:** also known as cookies.

**BLACK ONION SEEDS:** see SEEDS.

**BREADCRUMBS:**
Packaged: fine-textured, crunchy, purchased, white breadcrumbs.
Stale: one- or two-day-old bread made into crumbs by grating, blending or processing.

**BUTTER:** use salted or unsalted ("sweet") butter; 125g is equal to 1 stick butter.

**BUTTERMILK:** low-fat milk cultured with bacteria to give it a slightly sour, tangy taste; low-fat yogurt can be substituted.

**CAJUN SEASONING:** used to impart a traditional spicy Cajun flavour to fried foods; this packaged blend of assorted herbs and spices can include paprika, basil, onion, cayenne, fennel, thyme or tarragon.

**CANNELLINI BEANS:** small, dried white bean similar in appearance and flavour to other *phaseolus vulgaris*: great northern, navy and haricot beans.

**CAPERS:** the grey-green buds of a warm-climate (usually Mediterranean) shrub sold either dried and salted, or pickled in a vinegar brine; used to enhance sauces and dressings with their piquancy.

**CAPSICUM:** also known as bell pepper or, simply, pepper. Seeds and membranes should be discarded before use.

**CARDAMOM:** native to India and used extensively in its cuisine; can be purchased in pod, seed or ground form. Has a distinctive aromatic, sweetly rich flavour and is one of the world's most expensive spices.

**CHEESE:**
**Blue vein:** mould-treated cheese mottled with blue veining; many varieties, ranging from firm, crumbly and strong-flavoured to mild, creamy and brie-like.

**Bocconcini:** small rounds of fresh "baby" mozzarella, a delicate, semi-soft, white cheese traditionally made in Italy from buffalo's milk. Spoils rapidly so must be kept under refrigeration, in brine, for 1 or 2 days at most.

**Brie:** buttery soft cheese with an edible, chalk-like, white-mould rind; originally from France but now manufactured locally. Very high fat content; when ripe and ready to eat, the centre of this cheese should be quite runny.

**Cheddar:** the most common cow's milk "tasty" cheese; should be aged, hard and have a pronounced bite flavour.

**Fetta:** Greek in origin; a crumbly goat's or sheep's milk cheese with a sharp, salty taste.

**Gruyere:** a Swiss cheese having small holes and a nutty, slightly salty flavour.

**Parmesan:** a sharp-tasting, dry, hard cheese, made from skim or part skim milk and aged for at least a year before being sold. The best quality is Parmigiano Reggiano, from Italy, aged a minimum of three years.

**Ricotta:** a sweet, fairly moist, fresh curd cheese having a low-fat content.

**CHICKPEAS:** also called garbanzos, hummus or channa; an irregularly round, sandy-coloured legume used extensively in Mediterranean and Latin cooking.

**CHILLIES:** available in many different types and sizes. Use rubber gloves when seeding and chopping to avoid burning your skin. Discard seeds to lessen the heat level.

**Powder:** the Asian variety is the hottest, made from ground chillies; it can be used as a substitute for fresh chillies in the proportion of 1/2 teaspoon ground chilli powder to 1 medium chopped fresh chilli.

**Sauce:** our recipes used a hot Chinese variety made of chillies, salt and vinegar. Use sparingly, increasing amounts to taste.

**Sweet chilli sauce:** a comparatively mild, Thai-type, commercial sauce made from red chillies, sugar, garlic and vinegar.

**CHINESE BROCCOLI:** also known as gai lum.

**CHINESE CABBAGE:** also known as Peking cabbage or wong bok.

**CHINESE WATER SPINACH:** also known as swamp spinach, ung choy, kang kong.

**CHOY SUM:** also known as flowering bok choy or flowering white cabbage.

**COCONUT:**
**Cream:** available in cans and cartons; made from coconut meat and water.

Pistachios

Pine nuts

Pecans

Slivered
almonds

Flaked
almonds

Macadamias

**Milk:** pure, unsweetened; available in cans.

**CORIANDER:** also known as cilantro or Chinese parsley; bright-green, leafy herb with a pungent flavour. Often stirred into a dish just before serving for maximum impact.

**CORNFLOUR:** also known as cornstarch; used as a thickening agent in cooking.

**COUSCOUS:** a fine, grain-like cereal product, originally from North Africa; made of semolina.

**CREAM:** fresh pouring cream (minimum fat content 35%).

**Sour:** a thick, commercially cultured soured cream (minimum fat content 35%).

**CREME FRAICHE:** a fresh matured cream that has been commercially lightly soured (minimum fat content 35%); available in cartons from delicatessens and supermarkets. To make creme fraiche, combine 300ml cream with 300ml sour cream in bowl; cover, stand at room temperature until mixture thickens. This will take 1 or 2 days, depending on room temperature; refrigerate once fermented. Makes about 2½ cups (625ml).

**CURRY LEAVES:** shiny, bright-green, sharp-ended leaves used, fresh or dried, in cooking, especially in Indian curries.

**CURRY PASTE:** some recipes in this book call for commercially prepared pastes of various strengths and flavours, ranging from the mild Tikka and medium Madras to the fiery Vindaloo. Use whichever one you feel suits your spice-level tolerance.

**DHAL:** an Indian term that describes both legumes, dried peas and beans, and the range of spicy, stew-like dishes containing them.

**EGGPLANT:** also known as aubergine.

**EGGS:** some recipes in this book call for raw or barely cooked eggs; exercise caution if there is a salmonella problem in your area.

**ENGLISH SPINACH:** correct name for spinach; the green vegetable often called spinach is correctly known as silverbeet (see separate chapter).

**FENNEL:** also known as finocchio or anise.

**FETTUCCINE:** A ribbon pasta, about 5mm in width, made from durum wheat semolina and egg, available fresh or dried, plain or flavoured with herbs, pepper or vegetable essences.

**FISH SAUCE:** also called nam pla or nuoc nam; made from pulverised, salted, fermented fish, most often anchovies. Has a pungent smell and strong taste; use sparingly. There are many different fish sauces on the market, and the intensity of flavour varies.

**FIVE-SPICE POWDER:** a fragrant mixture of ground cinnamon, cloves, star anise, Sichuan pepper and fennel seeds.

**FLOUR, PLAIN:** also called all-purpose flour.

**GARAM MASALA:** a blend of spices, originally from Northern India, based on cardamom, cinnamon, cloves, coriander and cumin. Sometimes chilli is added.

**GARLIC:** a bulb contains many cloves which can be crushed, sliced, chopped, or used whole, peeled or unpeeled.

**GELATINE:** (also called gelatin) the recipes in this book use powdered gelatine. It is also available in sheet form, called leaf gelatine.

**GHEE:** clarified butter; with the milk solids removed, this semi-solid fat can be heated to a high temperature without burning.

**GHERKIN:** also known as cornichon; both the name of a kind of tiny, young, dark-green cucumber and the term to describe it after it has been pickled with herbs in vinegar.

**GINGER:**

**Fresh:** also known as green or root ginger; the thick gnarled root of a tropical plant. Can be kept, peeled, in dry sherry in a jar and refrigerated, or frozen in an airtight container.

**Pickled pink:** available, packaged, from Asian groceries; pickled, paper-thin shavings of ginger in a mixture of vinegar, sugar and natural colouring.

**HERBS:** when specified, we used 1 teaspoon dried (not ground) herbs as being the equivalent of 4 teaspoons (1 tablespoon) chopped fresh herbs.

**HOISIN SAUCE:** a thick, sweet and spicy Chinese paste made from salted, fermented soy beans, onions and garlic; used as a marinade or baste, or to accent stir-fries and barbecued or roasted foods.

**HORSERADISH CREAM:** a creamy paste of grated horseradish, vinegar, oil and sugar, often used as a condiment.

**KALONJI:** see SEEDS

**KITCHEN STRING:** be certain to use string made from a natural material specifically for use in cooking; a synthetic string will melt if used over heat or in the oven.

**LEMON GRASS:** a tall, clumping, lemon-smelling and tasting, sharp-edged grass; the white lower part of each stem is chopped and used in Asian cooking or for making tea.

**MAPLE SYRUP:** distilled sap of the maple tree. Maple-flavoured syrup or pancake syrup is made from cane sugar and artificial maple flavouring; is a poor substitute for the real thing.

**MIRIN:** a sweet, low-alcohol rice wine used in Japanese cooking; sometimes referred to as simply as rice wine. Do not confuse with sake, the Japanese rice wine made for drinking.

**MORTADELLA:** a delicately spiced and smoked Italian sausage made of pork, beef and pork fat.

**MUSTARD, SEEDED:** a coarse-grain mustard made of crushed mustard seeds and Dijon-style French mustard.

**NOODLES, FRIED:** Crispy egg noodles, packaged (commonly a 100g packet).

**NUTS:**

**Almonds:** Blanched, skins removed; Flaked, paper-thin slices; Ground, also called almond meal; Slivered, small lengthways-cut pieces.

**Hazelnuts:** also known as filberts; plump, grape-size, rich, sweet nut having a brown inedible skin that is removed by rubbing heated nuts together vigorously in a teatowel.

**Macadamias:** native to Australia and now grown extensively in Hawaii. A rich, buttery nut that should be stored in the refrigerator because of its high oil content.

**Pecans:** native to the United States and now grown locally; golden-brown, buttery and rich. Good in savoury as well as sweet dishes; especially good in salads.

**Pine:** also called pignoli; small, cream-coloured kernels obtained from the cones of different varieties of pine trees.

**Pistachios:** pale-green, delicately flavoured nut inside a hard, off-white shell. To peel, soak shelled nuts in boiling water for about 5 minutes; drain, then pat dry with absorbent paper. Rub skins with cloth to peel.

**OIL:**

**Hazelnut:** a mono-unsaturated oil, made in France, extracted from crushed hazelnuts.

**Macadamia:** a mono-unsaturated oil extracted from macadamia nuts.

**Olive:** a mono-unsaturated oil, made from the pressing of tree-ripened olives; especially good for everyday cooking and in salad dressings. Extra Light or Light Olive Oil describes the mild flavour of the oil and has nothing to do with fat levels.

**Peanut:** pressed from ground peanuts; good for stir-frying because of its high smoke point.

**Sesame:** used throughout Southeast Asia; made from roasted, crushed white sesame seeds and used as a flavouring rather than a cooking medium.

**Vegetable:** any of a number of oils having a plant rather than an animal source.

Cannellini beans

Dried chilli flakes

Fresh red serrano chilli

Fresh ginger

Pickled pink ginger

Glace ginger

*Chinese dried mushrooms*

*Pancetta*

*Pastrami*

*Pawpaw*

*V-slicer*

*Savarin*

**ONION FLAKES:** packaged (usually in 55g packets) chopped and dehydrated white onion pieces; a garnish more than an ingredient.

**OYSTER SAUCE:** Asian in origin; a concentrated dark-brown sauce made from oysters, brine and soy sauce, and thickened with starches.

**PANCETTA:** an Italian salt-cured pork roll, usually cut from the belly; used diced in many dishes to add flavour. Substitute bacon.

**PAPRIKA:** ground, dried red capsicum (bell pepper), available sweet or hot.

**PASTA SAUCE, BOTTLED:** a prepared tomato-based sauce (sometimes called ragu or sugo on the label) sold in supermarkets.

**PASTRAMI:** a highly seasoned, cured and smoked beef, usually cut from the round; ready to eat when purchased.

**PAWPAW:** also known as papaya or papaw; large, pear-shaped, red-orange tropical fruit. Sometime used unripe (green) in cooking.

**PEARL BARLEY:** barley which has had its outer husk (bran) removed, and then steamed and polished before being used in cooking.

**PITTA:** also known as pita, Lebanese bread or pocket bread; a Middle Eastern, wheat-flour bread, usually sold pre-packaged in large, flat pieces easily separated into two paper-thin rounds. Comes in smaller, thicker pieces commonly called Pocket Pitta.

**PLUM SAUCE:** a thick, sweet and sour, prepared dipping sauce made from plums, vinegar, sugar, chillies and spices.

**POLENTA:** a flour-like cereal made from ground corn (maize); similar to cornmeal but coarser and darker in colour; also the name given to the dish made from it.

**PROSCIUTTO:** salted-cured, air-dried (unsmoked) pressed ham; usually sold in paper-thin slices, ready to eat.

**REDCURRANT JELLY:** a preserve made from redcurrants used as glaze for desserts or as a sauce ingredient.

**RICE:**

**Arborio:** small, round grain, especially able to absorb a great deal of liquid, as in a risotto.

**Calrose:** a medium-grain rice that is extremely versatile; can substitute for short- or long-grain rice if necessary.

**Long-grain:** elongated grain, remains separate when cooked; Asia's choice for steaming.

**SAFFRON:** stigma of a member of the crocus family, available in strands or ground form; imparts a yellow-orange colour to food once infused. Quality varies greatly; the best is the most expensive food in the world. Should be stored in the freezer.

**SAMBAL OELEK:** (also ulek or olek) Indonesian in origin; a salty paste made from ground chillies, sugar and spices.

**SAVARIN PAN:** a heatproof ring mould named after the baba-like, rum-soaked, rich yeast cake for which it was designed; its use has been extended to include uncooked recipes requiring ring moulds, such as a jelly mould.

**SEEDS:**

**Black Onion:** also kalonji or nigella.

**Mustard, Black:** also brown mustard seeds.

**Mustard, Yellow:** also white mustard seeds.

**SEMOLINA:** made from durum wheat milled into granules of various sizes and textures; used as a cereal and in desserts.

**SOY SAUCE:** made from fermented soy beans. Several different types are available in supermarkets and Asian food stores, among them salt-reduced, light, sweet and salty.

**SUGAR:** the recipes in this book used coarse granulated table sugar, also known as crystal sugar, unless otherwise specified.

**Brown:** a soft, fine granulated sugar containing molasses to give it its characteristic colour.

**Caster:** also known as superfine or finely granulated table sugar.

**SUMAC:** a purple-red, astringent spice ground from berries growing on shrubs that flourish wild around the Mediterranean and even further East to Iran, where it is sprinkled over the national dish of grilled meat and steamed rice. Good in salad dressings and sauces.

**TACO SEASONING MIX:** a packaged Mexican seasoning mix made from oregano, cumin, chillies and various other spices.

**TAHINI:** a rich, buttery paste made from crushed sesame seeds.

**TAMARIND CONCENTRATE:** a thick, purple-black, ready-to-use, sweet-sour paste extracted from the pulp of pods from tamarind trees; use as is, with no soaking, stirred into casseroles and stews.

**TOMATO:**

**Paste:** a concentrated tomato puree used to flavour soups, stews, sauces and casseroles.

**Puree:** canned pureed tomatoes (not a concentrate). Use fresh, peeled, pureed tomatoes as a substitute.

**Sun-dried:** dehydrated tomatoes. The recipes in this book use sun-dried tomatoes packaged in oil unless otherwise specified.

**TURMERIC:** a member of the ginger family; its root is dried and ground, resulting in the rich yellow powder that gives many Indian dishes their characteristic colour. It is intensely pungent in taste but not hot.

**V-SLICER:** The German company Börner's tradename for an efficient kitchen tool having three different blades to slice, dice and shred vegetables and fruits. Caution is advised when hand-operating this extremely sharp instrument; a mandoline, the generic Italian slicer, or the various cutting discs of a food processor, can be substituted.

**VINEGAR:**

**Balsamic:** authentic only from the province of Modena, Italy; made from a regional wine of white Trebbiano grapes specially processed then aged in antique wooden casks to give the exquisitely piquant flavour.

**Brown malt:** made from fermented malt and beech shavings.

**Cider:** made from fermented apples.

**Red wine:** based on fermented red wine.

**Rice:** made from fermented rice, colourless and flavoured with sugar and salt.

**White wine:** made from fermented white wine.

**WASABI:** a Japanese green horseradish paste; sharp and biting so a little goes a very long way.

**WATER CHESTNUTS:** resembling a chestnut, hence its English name; a small, brown tuber peeled to reveal its crisp, white, nutty-tasting flesh. The crunchy texture is best experienced fresh, however, canned water chestnuts are more easily obtained and can be kept about a month, once opened, under refrigeration.

**WATERCRESS:** small, crisp, deep-green, rounded leaves having a slightly bitter, peppery flavour. Good in mixed salads, soups and sandwiches.

**YOGURT:** unflavoured, full-fat cow's milk yogurt has been used in these recipes unless otherwise specified. Besides being eaten on its own, yogurt is used in cooking to tenderise and thicken, and is also an ingredient in sauces, dressings and desserts.

**ZUCCHINI:** also known as courgettes.

# Index

# Make your own stock

These stock recipes can be made up to 4 days ahead and stored, covered, in the refrigerator. Be sure to remove any fat from the surface after the cooled stock has been refrigerated overnight. If the stock is to be kept longer, it is best to freeze it in smaller quantities. Stock is also available in cans or tetra packs. Stock cubes or powder can be used. As a guide, 1 teaspoon of stock powder or 1 small crumbled stock cube mixed with 1 cup (250ml) water will give a fairly strong stock. You should be aware of the salt and fat content of stock cubes, powders and prepared stocks.

**Fish Stock**
**1.5kg fish bones**
**3 litres (12 cups) water**
**1 medium (150g) onion,
  chopped**
**2 sticks celery, chopped**
**2 bay leaves**
**1 teaspoon black
  peppercorns**
Combine all ingredients in large pan; simmer, uncovered, 20 minutes. Strain.

**Chicken Stock**
**2kg chicken bones**
**2 medium (300g) onions,
  chopped**
**2 sticks celery, chopped**
**2 medium (250g) carrots,
  chopped**
**3 bay leaves**
**2 teaspoons black
  peppercorns**
**5 litres (20 cups) water**
Combine all ingredients in large pan; simmer, uncovered, 2 hours. Strain.

**Beef Stock**
**2kg meaty beef bones**
**2 medium (300g) onions**
**2 sticks celery, chopped**
**2 medium (250g) carrots,
  chopped**
**3 bay leaves**
**2 teaspoons black
  peppercorns**
**5 litres (20 cups) water**
**3 litres (12 cups) water, extra**
Place bones and unpeeled chopped onions in baking dish. Bake in hot oven about 1 hour or until bones and onions are well browned. Transfer bones and onions to large pan; add celery, carrots, bay leaves, peppercorns and the water. Simmer, uncovered, 3 hours. Add the extra water; simmer, uncovered, further 1 hour. Strain.

**Vegetable Stock**
**2 large (360g) carrots,
  chopped**
**2 large (360g) parsnips,
  chopped**
**4 medium (600g) onions,
  chopped**
**12 sticks celery, chopped**
**4 bay leaves**
**2 teaspoons black
  peppercorns**
**6 litres (24 cups) water**
Combine all ingredients in large pan; simmer, uncovered, 1½ hours. Strain.

*All stock recipes make about 2.5 litres (10 cups).*

# QUICK CONVERSION GUIDE

Wherever you live in the world you can use our recipes with the help of our easy-to-follow conversions for all your cooking needs. These conversions are approximate only. The difference between the exact and approximate conversion of liquid and dry measures amounts to only a teaspoon or two, and will not make any difference to your cooking results.

## MEASURING EQUIPMENT

The difference between measuring cups internationally is minimal within 2 or 3 teaspoons' difference. (For the record, 1 Australian metric measuring cup will hold approximately 250ml.) The most accurate way of measuring dry ingredients is to weigh them. When measuring liquids use a clear glass or plastic jug with the metric markings.

If you would like the measuring cups and spoons as used in our Test Kitchen, turn to page 128 for details and order coupon. In this book we use metric measuring cups and spoons approved by Standards Australia.

● a graduated set of four cups for measuring dry ingredients; the sizes are marked on the cups.
● a graduated set of four spoons for measuring dry and liquid ingredients; the amounts are marked on the spoons.
● 1 TEASPOON: 5ml
● 1 TABLESPOON: 20ml.

### NOTE: NZ, CANADA, USA AND UK ALL USE 15ml TABLESPOONS.
### ALL CUP AND SPOON MEASUREMENTS ARE LEVEL.

## DRY MEASURES

| METRIC | IMPERIAL |
|---|---|
| 15g | 1/2oz |
| 30g | 1oz |
| 60g | 2oz |
| 90g | 3oz |
| 125g | 4oz (1/4lb) |
| 155g | 5oz |
| 185g | 6oz |
| 220g | 7oz |
| 250g | 8oz (1/2lb) |
| 280g | 9oz |
| 315g | 10oz |
| 345g | 11oz |
| 375g | 12oz (3/4lb) |
| 410g | 13oz |
| 440g | 14oz |
| 470g | 15oz |
| 500g | 16oz (1lb) |
| 750g | 24oz (11/2lb) |
| 1kg | 32oz (2lb) |

## LIQUID MEASURES

| METRIC | IMPERIAL |
|---|---|
| 30ml | 1 fluid oz |
| 60ml | 2 fluid oz |
| 100ml | 3 fluid oz |
| 125ml | 4 fluid oz |
| 150ml | 5 fluid oz (1/4 pint/1 gill) |
| 190ml | 6 fluid oz |
| 250ml | 8 fluid oz |
| 300ml | 10 fluid oz (1/2 pint) |
| 500ml | 16 fluid oz |
| 600ml | 20 fluid oz (1 pint) |
| 1000ml (1 litre) | 13/4 pints |

### WE USE LARGE EGGS WITH AN AVERAGE WEIGHT OF 60g

## HELPFUL MEASURES

| METRIC | IMPERIAL |
|---|---|
| 3mm | 1/8in |
| 6mm | 1/4in |
| 1cm | 1/2in |
| 2cm | 3/4in |
| 2.5cm | 1in |
| 5cm | 2in |
| 6cm | 21/2in |
| 8cm | 3in |
| 10cm | 4in |
| 13cm | 5in |
| 15cm | 6in |
| 18cm | 7in |
| 20cm | 8in |
| 23cm | 9in |
| 25cm | 10in |
| 28cm | 11in |
| 30cm | 12in (1ft) |

## HOW TO MEASURE

When using the graduated metric measuring cups, it is important to shake the dry ingredients loosely into the required cup. Do not tap the cup on the bench, or pack the ingredients into the cup unless otherwise directed. Level top of cup with knife. When using graduated metric measuring spoons, level top of spoon with knife. When measuring liquids in the jug, place jug on flat surface, check for accuracy at eye level.

## OVEN TEMPERATURES

These oven temperatures are only a guide; we've given you the lower degree of heat. Always check the manufacturer's manual.

| | C° (Celsius) | F° (Fahrenheit) | Gas Mark |
|---|---|---|---|
| Very slow | 120 | 250 | 1 |
| Slow | 150 | 300 | 2 |
| Moderately slow | 160 | 325 | 3 |
| Moderate | 180 - 190 | 350 - 375 | 4 |
| Moderately hot | 200 - 210 | 400 - 425 | 5 |
| Hot | 220 - 230 | 450 - 475 | 6 |
| Very hot | 240 - 250 | 500 - 525 | 7 |